Exploring History

for Bilingual Classes SII

Conflict in the Middle East

Author
Dr. Alfred Schlicht

Contributors
Dr. Deanna Nebert
Dr. Ulrich Baumgärtner

Editor
Dr. Christa Lohmann

westermann

Eine kommentierte Linkliste befindet sich unter:
www.westermann.de/geschichte-linkliste

Druck A[1] / Jahr 2011
Alle Drucke der Serie A sind im Unterricht parallel verwendbar.

Redaktion: Christoph Meyer, Dorle Bennöhr
Herstellung: Udo Sauter
Typografie: Thomas Schröder
Satz: Ottomedien, Hanhofen
Druck und Bindung: westermann druck GmbH, Braunschweig

ISBN 978-3-14-**111100**-2

Jewish Settlers in Palestine, 1925

Leaders of the Arab Uprising in Palestine, 1938

"Palestine", cartoon

Israeli Declaration of Independence, 1948

Protest in Palestine, 2002

Israeli-Palestinian Demonstration, Tel Aviv, 2002

Conflict in the Middle East

The conflict in the Middle East between Israel and the Arab states is an extraordinarily complex historical phenomenon: It has its deepest roots in antiquity and in European anti-Semitism. It is part of Jewish as well as Arab history. European imperialism, Arab nationalism and Jewish Zionism all played significant roles at its inception. The conflict, originally a pure conflict of interests over mutually exclusive demands, was intensified by ideological and radical instrumentalization on both sides. At the same time the Middle East conflict is a paradigm of historical globalization.

We cannot be indifferent to world developments that at first appear to be concentrated in regions far away. As the Middle East conflict has demonstrated first and foremost, we have to try to understand global historical contexts. At the same time the Middle East conflict proves that current problems can only be understood when we comprehend their historical dimensions. Seen only from today the reasons for the Middle East conflict as well as the motives of its main players cannot be grasped – only when we consider its history can we understand our role in this conflict. Even in the 21st century the Middle East conflict remains a prominent flashpoint on the world agenda, as has been shown by the priority given to it by US President Barack Obama. He, like several of his predecessors, has realized that peace in the Middle East must remain a primary goal for the leading world power. The European Union also has vital interests in the region and contributes to its stabilization.

A Dream and a Promise

M 1 **Theodor Herzl** (1860–1904), Author and Zionist, Photograph, about 1900

Zionism

The historical development leading to the Middle East conflict has its roots in the late nineteenth century. In 1896 Theodor Herzl, an Austrian Jew, published "The Jewish State" ("Der Judenstaat") in which he outlined the idea of a Jewish state as an "effort to solve the Jewish question". Under the impression of the Dreyfus affair in which a Jewish army officer suffered harsh discrimination, Herzl became convinced that only a Jewish state could end discrimination and persecution. As long as Jews lived as minorities in Christian (and other) societies they were always threatened by attack, persecution, discrimination or loss of identity through assimilation. Indeed, assimilation was the goal in Western European societies. Only a Jewish state could guarantee Jewish survival without dangers and risks. There were, according to Herzl, different possibilities for the geographic location of such a state: It could be founded in Argentina, Uganda, Madagascar, or – the best solution – in the historic home of the Jews, in Palestine. Herzl initiated and led the First Zionist Congress in Basel, Switzerland, in 1897. He summed the congress up with the words: "At Basel I founded the Jewish state." Few at that time would have thought he was right.

Herzl did not see the problem of people already living in the area who might oppose the founding of a Jewish state on territory which they considered their own. In a utopian novel "Altneuland" (1902) he presented an idealized picture of the Jewish state as it might take shape in future. Political Zionism developed only slowly. For centuries Jews had immigrated to Palestine to live close to the holy places of their religion and their forefathers. Numbers increased somewhat in the nineteenth century, when many Jews left Russia (2.6 million between 1882 and 1914) and Eastern Europe under the pressure of pogroms and discrimination. However, few wished to go to Palestine, in those days a remote province of the Ottoman Empire. The favourite destinations of Jewish emigrants were Western Europe, America or South Africa.

British Promises

The political Zionists relentlessly sought support from one of the then Great Powers. The German Kaiser as well as the Ottoman Sultan opposed the idea. During the First World War the British sympathized more with the Zionist project. A Jewish state or even a Jewish community – whatever character the envisaged "national home" assumed – could stabilize British interests and influence along the Suez Canal and in the Eastern Mediterranean. Therefore, the British officially supported the ideas of Zionism.

However, Britain was forced to commit herself to various strategies during World War I. On the one hand, an Arab revolt against Ottoman domination was *sparked* to weaken Turkish and German influence in the Middle East. In return the Arabs were vaguely promised an Arab national state to be founded after the war and the ensuing dismantling of the Ottoman Empire (the McMahon Letter). On the other hand, Britain and France attempted to establish and maintain their spheres of influence in the region. These were formally stated in the Sykes-Picot Agreement of 1916. The Balfour Declaration of 1917, in which

to spark: to make sth. happen

British Foreign Secretary Balfour promised Lord Rothschild to support a Jewish national home, sealed the fate of the Middle East in a third document.

These three documents aroused unease and distrust – especially among Arabs. Promises were made and commitments signed to satisfy all sides – though in spirit the documents were incompatible.

The Situation after World War I

After the First World War the Ottoman Empire was dissolved. Its former Arab provinces came under French and British mandate. Hashemite rulers were entrusted with the newly founded states of Iraq (in Mesopotamia) and Jordan (east of the Jordan River) in order to meet Arab expectations, at least partially. A comprehensive "Arab empire", a national state for all or a majority of Arabs, was not in sight; Arab expectations were frustrated. Palestine (west of the Jordan River) came under British administration.

Jewish Immigration

From 1882 to 1903 only about 30,000 Jews immigrated to Palestine. In 1914 around 40,000 Jews lived there (out of a total population of 720,000). This was far too few to found a "Jewish state". In fact, there was no urgent need to create such a state. In those days it seemed to be a utopian vision rather than a real option or – as it later proved to be – a sheer necessity. The term used in the programme of the Zionist Congress of Basel in 1897 as well as in the Balfour Declaration of 1917 was "national home".

M 2 **Population in Palestine before World War I**

1880	1914
240,000 (including 13,000 Jews)	720,000 (including 39,000 Jews and 600,000 Muslims)

With Palestine under British control, Zionists continued their efforts to realize the goal that had been set in Basel. When the San Remo Conference assigned the Mandate for Palestine to Britain, a decision confirmed by the Council of the League of Nations in the summer of 1922, the conference resolution was "in favour of the establishment in Palestine of a national home for the Jewish people", whereas "nothing should be done which might prejudice the ... rights of existing non-Jewish communities".

M 3 **Jewish Settlers in Palestine,** 1925

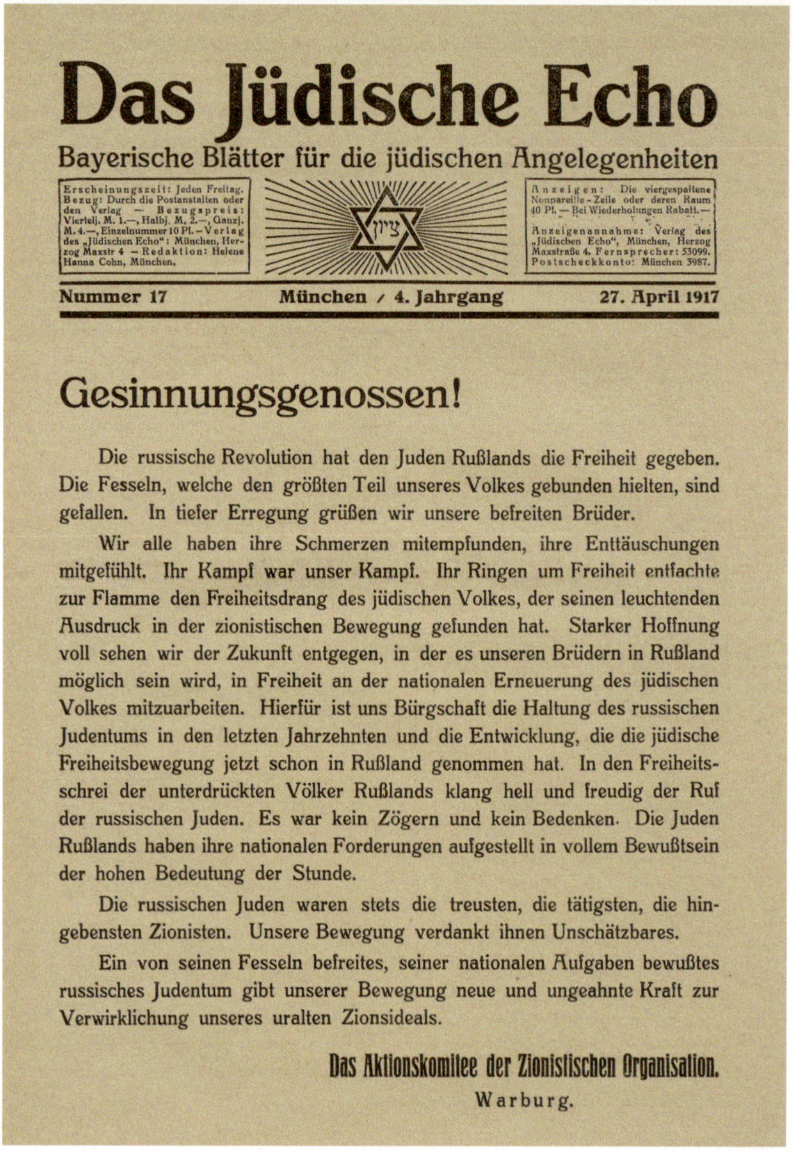

Das Jüdische Echo

Bayerische Blätter für die jüdischen Angelegenheiten

Erscheinungszeit: Jeden Freitag. Bezug: Durch die Postanstalten oder den Verlag — Bezugspreis: Viertelj. M. 1.—, Halbj. M. 2.—, Ganzj. M. 4.—, Einzelnummer 10 Pf. – Verlag des „Jüdischen Echo": München, Herzog Maxstr 4 — Redaktion: Helene Hanna Cohn, München.

ציון

Anzeigen: Die viergespaltene Nonpareille-Zeile oder deren Raum 40 Pf. — Bei Wiederholungen Rabatt. —

Anzeigenannahme: Verlag des „Jüdischen Echo", München, Herzog Maxstraße 4. Fernsprecher: 53099. Postscheckkonto: München 3987.

Nummer 17 München / 4. Jahrgang 27. April 1917

Gesinnungsgenossen!

Die russische Revolution hat den Juden Rußlands die Freiheit gegeben. Die Fesseln, welche den größten Teil unseres Volkes gebunden hielten, sind gefallen. In tiefer Erregung grüßen wir unsere befreiten Brüder.

Wir alle haben ihre Schmerzen mitempfunden, ihre Enttäuschungen mitgefühlt. Ihr Kampf war unser Kampf. Ihr Ringen um Freiheit entfachte zur Flamme den Freiheitsdrang des jüdischen Volkes, der seinen leuchtenden Ausdruck in der zionistischen Bewegung gefunden hat. Starker Hoffnung voll sehen wir der Zukunft entgegen, in der es unseren Brüdern in Rußland möglich sein wird, in Freiheit an der nationalen Erneuerung des jüdischen Volkes mitzuarbeiten. Hierfür ist uns Bürgschaft die Haltung des russischen Judentums in den letzten Jahrzehnten und die Entwicklung, die die jüdische Freiheitsbewegung jetzt schon in Rußland genommen hat. In den Freiheitsschrei der unterdrückten Völker Rußlands klang hell und freudig der Ruf der russischen Juden. Es war kein Zögern und kein Bedenken. Die Juden Rußlands haben ihre nationalen Forderungen aufgestellt in vollem Bewußtsein der hohen Bedeutung der Stunde.

Die russischen Juden waren stets die treusten, die tätigsten, die hingebensten Zionisten. Unsere Bewegung verdankt ihnen Unschätzbares.

Ein von seinen Fesseln befreites, seiner nationalen Aufgaben bewußtes russisches Judentum gibt unserer Bewegung neue und ungeahnte Kraft zur Verwirklichung unseres uralten Zionsideals.

Das Aktionskomitee der Zionistischen Organisation.
Warburg.

M 4 "The Jewish Echo"
Introduction to the Edition of 27 April 1917

Palestinian and Arab Nationalism

In 1922 Palestine had 816,000 inhabitants, nearly 84,000 of whom were Jewish. But as Jews started to construct their own infrastructure and made preparations which seemed to lead more to a Jewish state than to a "national home", Palestinian consciousness was raised. Palestinian "nationalism" began to take shape, especially as the future of the proposed "Arab Empire" seemed more removed and theoretical than in the last years of the Ottoman Empire. Regional "nationalisms" developed in the Arab world – Palestinian nationalism was catalysed by Jewish "nationalism" or Zionism. More and more the British faced a double challenge in Palestine: On the one hand, Jewish efforts to promote immigration became particularly intense in 1933 when the National Socialists under Hitler assumed power in Germany.

On the other hand, Arab resistance to Jewish immigration grew. A civil war with different fronts erupted: Jews and Arabs against the British and against each other. The situation deteriorated from year to

M 5 **Leaders of the Arab Uprising in Palestine,** 1938

year. As Jewish immigration quickly increased, Arabs felt their position threatened and provoked disturbances which were countered violently by the British.

A full-scale Arab revolt against the Jews and the British broke out in 1936. David Ben Gurion, who later became Israel's first president, summed up the conflict in clear and simple terms: "We and they want the same thing: We both want Palestine. And that is the fundamental conflict."

A Royal Commission under Lord Peel presented a report in 1937, stating that Arab opposition to the founding of a Jewish state and the Arab desire for national independence were the causes underlying the revolt. The commission recommended the separation of Palestine into two states – one Arab, one Jewish. The plan was accepted by the Jews, but rejected by the Arabs. Despite initially favouring the plan, the British government eventually rejected it in 1938.

The White Paper

Nevertheless, the British needed a comprehensive solution to the Palestine problem. A conference in London in February/March 1939 provided the stage on which the British government announced its new policy, published in a White Paper: Jewish immigration to Palestine was severely restricted, it should cease altogether after five years, and purchase of land by Jews should be limited.

"Although it is not difficult *to contend* that the large number of Jewish immigrants who have been admitted so far have been absorbed economically, the fear of the Arabs that this influx will continue indefinitely until the Jewish population is in a position to dominate them has produced consequences which are extremely grave for Jews and Arabs alike and for the peace and prosperity of Palestine" (British Government: The White Paper, 17 May 1939).

Both Jews and Arabs rejected the White Paper.

to contend: to claim sth. is true

"The Jewish State" – A Dream

M 6 "The Jewish State"

Theodor Herzl writes in his famous book (1896):

I believe that I understand Anti-Semitism, which is really a highly complex movement. I consider it from a Jewish standpoint, yet without fear or hatred. I believe that I can see what elements there are in it of vulgar sport, of common trade jealousy, of inherited prejudice, of religious intolerance, and also of pretended self-defence. I think the Jewish question is no more a social than a religious one, notwithstanding that it sometimes takes these and other forms. It is a national question, which can only be solved by making it a political world-question to be discussed and settled by the civilised nations of the world in council.

We are a people – one people.

We have honestly endeavoured everywhere to merge ourselves in the social life of surrounding communities and to preserve only the faith of our fathers. We are not permitted to do so. In vain are we loyal patriots, our loyalty in some places running to extremes; in vain do we make the same sacrifices of life and property as our fellow-citizens; in vain do we strive to increase the fame of our native land in science and art, or her wealth by trade and commerce. [...]

We are one people – our enemies have made us one *in our despite,* as repeatedly happens in history. Distress binds us together, and, thus united, we suddenly discover our strength. Yes, we are strong enough to form a State, and, indeed, a model State. We possess all human and material resources necessary for the purpose. [...]

The whole plan is in its essence perfectly simple, as it must necessarily be if it is to come within the comprehension of all. Let the sovereignty be granted us over a portion of the globe large enough to satisfy the rightful requirements of a nation; the rest we shall manage for ourselves. [...]

The plan, simple in design, but complicated in execution, will be carried out by two agencies: The Society of Jews and the Jewish Company. The Society of Jews will do the preparatory work in the domains of science and politics, which the Jewish Company will afterwards practically apply. The Jewish Company will see to the realisation of the business interests of departing Jews, and will organise commerce and trade in the new country.

[...] Those Jews who agree with our idea of a State will attach themselves to the Society, which will thereby be authorised to confer and treat with Governments in the name of our people. The Society will thus be acknowledged in its relations with Governments as a State-creating power. This acknowledgment will practically create the State.

[...] Here two territories come under consideration, Palestine and Argentina. [...] Argentina is one of the most fertile countries in the world, extends over a vast area, has a sparse population and a mild climate. The Argentine Republic would derive considerable profit from the *cession* of a portion of its territory to us. The present infiltration of Jews has certainly produced some discontent, and it would be necessary to enlighten the Republic on the intrinsic difference of our new movement.

Palestine is our ever-memorable historic home. The very name of Palestine would attract our people with a force of marvellous potency. If His Majesty the Sultan were to give us Palestine, we could in return undertake to regulate the whole finances of Turkey. We should there form a portion of the *rampart* of Europe against Asia, an outpost of civilisation as opposed to barbarism. We should as a neutral State remain in contact with all Europe, which would have to guarantee our existence.

www.zionism-israel.com/js/Jewish_State_Chapter_1.html(and_2.html)

M 7 A Comment

Avi Shlaim, Israeli Historian and Professor for International Relationships in Oxford, on Theodor Herzl's ideas (2000):

Herzl himself exemplified the Zionist tendency to *indulge* in wishful thinking. He was certainly aware that Palestine was already populated with a substantial number of Arabs, although he was not particularly well informed about the social and economic conditions of the country. He viewed the natives as primitive and backward, and his attitude toward them was rather patronizing. He thought that as individuals they should enjoy full civil rights in a Jewish state but he did not consider them a society with collective political rights over the land in which they formed the overwhelming majority. Like many other early Zionists, Herzl hoped that economic benefits would reconcile the Arab population to the Zionist enterprise in Palestine. As the bearers of all the benefits of

Western civilization, the Jews, he thought, might be welcomed by the residents of the backward East. This optimistic forecast of Arab-Jewish relations in Palestine found its clearest expression in a novel published by Herzl in 1902 under the title Altneuland (Old-Newland). Rashid Bey, a spokesman for the native population, describes Jewish settlement as an unqualified blessing: "The Jews have made us prosperous, why should we be angry with them? They live with us as brothers, why should we not love them?" This picture, however, was nothing but a pipe dream, a Utopian fantasy. Its author completely overlooked the possibility that an Arab national movement would grow in Palestine in response to the Zionist drive to transform the country into a Jewish national home with a Jewish majority.

In defense of Herzl it should be pointed out that at the end of the nineteenth century Palestine was a province of the Ottoman Empire, and an Arab national movement was only beginning to develop there. Still, his preference for playing the game of high politics was unmistakable. His most persistent efforts were directed at persuading the Ottoman sultan to grant a *charter* for Jewish settlement and a Jewish homeland in Palestine. But he also approached many other world leaders and influential magnates for help in promoting his pet project. Among those who granted him an audience were the pope, the king of Italy, the German kaiser, and Joseph Chamberlain, the British colonial secretary. In each case Herzl presented his project in a manner best calculated to appeal to the listener: to the sultan he promised Jewish capital, to the kaiser he *intimated* that the Jewish territory would be an outpost of Berlin, to Chamberlain he held out the prospect that the Jewish territory would become a colony of the British Empire. Whatever the arguments used, Herzl's basic aim remained unchanged: obtaining the support of the great powers for turning Palestine into a political center for the Jewish people.

In its formative phase, under the direction of Herzl, the Zionist movement thus displayed two features that were to be of fundamental and enduring importance in its subsequent history: the nonrecognition of a Palestinian national entity, and the quest for an alliance with a great power external to the Middle East.

Avi Shlaim, The Iron Wall. Israel and the Arab World (London: W. W. Norton & Company, 2000), pp. 4–5.

in our despite: against our will
cession: the giving of land
rampart: e.g. a stone wall to protect a city or country
to indulge: to allow oneself sth.
charter: a document from a ruler granting rights
to intimate: to suggest

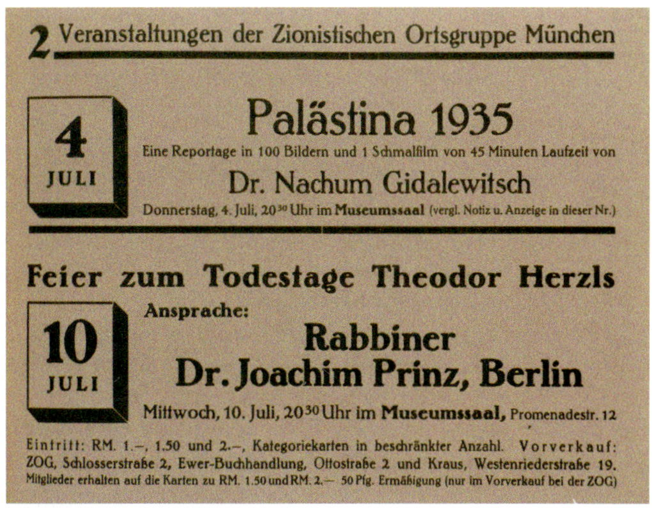

M 8 **"Palestine 1935"**
Poster of the Munich Zionist Group, 1935

Tasks

1. Portray the situation in Palestine at the beginning of the 20th century (text, M2).
2. Summarize the excerpt of Herzl's book, including the historical background of Zionism (text, M6).
3. Avi Shlaim criticizes and defends Herzl. Agree or disagree with him, giving reasons for your opinion (M7).
4. Comment on the consequences of Jewish immigration to Palestine, considering the appeal in the "The Jewish Echo" in your treatment (text, M2, M4, M8).

British Promises

M 9 The McMahon Letter

Sir Henry McMahon (1862–1949), British High Commissioner in Cairo, negotiated in 1915–16 with Hussein Ibn Ali, the Sherif of Mecca. The British government promised to support his bid for the restoration of the Caliphate (and leadership in the Arab world) if Hussein supported the British war effort against Turkey. Palestine was not mentioned by name in this exchange: the Arabs subsequently claimed that it had been included in the promise of an independent Arab state. The British denied this — as evidenced by McMahon's letter published in the London Times in 1937:

October 24, 1915 […]. I regret that you should have received from my last letter the impression that I regarded the question of limits and boundaries with coldness and hesitation; such was not the case, but it appeared to me that the time had not yet come when that question could be discussed in a conclusive manner.
I have realised, however, from your last letter that you regard this question as one of vital and urgent importance. I have, therefore, lost no time in informing the Government of Great Britain of the contents of your letter, and it is with great pleasure that I communicate to you on their behalf the following statement, which I am confident you will receive with satisfaction.
The two districts of Mersina and Alexandretta and portions of Syria lying to the west of the districts of Damascus, Horns, Hama and Aleppo cannot be said to be purely Arab, and should be excluded from the limits demanded.
With the above modification, and without prejudice to our existing treaties with Arab chiefs, we accept those limits.
As for those regions lying within those frontiers wherein Great Britain is free to act without *detriment* to the interests of her ally, France, I am empowered in the name of the Government of Great Britain to give the following assurances and make the following reply to your letter:
(1) Subject to the above modifications, Great Britain is prepared to recognise and support the independence of the Arabs in all the regions within the limits demanded by the Sherif of Mecca.
(2) Great Britain will guarantee the Holy Places against all external aggression and will recognise their inviolability.
(3) When the situation admits, Great Britain will give to the Arabs her advice and will assist them to establish what may appear to be the most suitable forms of government in those various territories.
(4) On the other hand, it is understood that the Arabs have decided to seek the advice and guidance of Great Britain only, and that such European advisers and officials as may be required for the formation of a sound form of administration will be British. […]
I am convinced that this declaration will assure you beyond all possible doubt of the sympathy of Great Britain towards the aspirations of her friends the Arabs and will result in a firm and lasting alliance, the immediate results of which will be the expulsion of the Turks from the Arab countries and the freeing of the Arab peoples from the Turkish yoke, which for so many years has pressed heavily upon them.

Walter Laqueur and Barry Rubin (eds.), The Israel-Arab Reader (New York: Penguin 2008), pp. 11–12.

M 10 The Sykes-Picot Agreement

Sir Mark Sykes (1873–1919), a distinguished British specialist in Middle Eastern studies, and Charles Georges-Picot, formerly French Consul in Beirut, prepared a draft agreement in 1915–16 about the post-war division of the Middle East, which was also approved in principle by Russia. Sir Edward Grey to Paul Cambon, 16 May 1916:

I have the honour to acknowledge the receipt of your Excellency's note of the 9th instant, stating that the French Government accept the limits of a future Arab State, or Confederation of States, and of those parts of Syria where French interests predominate, together with certain conditions attached thereto, such as they result from recent discussions in London and Petrograd on the subject.
I have the honour to inform your Excellency in reply that the acceptance of the whole project, as it now stands, will involve the *abdication* of considerable British interests, but, since His Majesty's Government recognise the advantage to the general cause of the Allies *entailed* in producing a more favourable internal political situation in Turkey, they are ready to accept the arrangement now arrived at, provided that the cooperation of the Arabs is secured, and that the

Arabs fulfill the conditions and obtain the towns of Horns, Hama, Damascus, and Aleppo.

It is accordingly understood between the French and British Governments –

1. That France and Great Britain are prepared to recognise and protect an independent Arab State or a Confederation of Arab States in the areas (A) and (B) marked on the annexed map [map not reproduced: Ed.] under the *suzerainty* of an Arab chief. That in area (A) France, and in area (B) Great Britain, shall have priority of right of enterprise and local loans. That in area (A) France, and in area (B) Great Britain, shall alone supply advisers or foreign functionaries at the request of the Arab State or Confederation of Arab States.

2. That in the blue area France, and in the red area Great Britain, shall be allowed to establish such direct or indirect administration or control as they desire and as they may think fit to arrange with the Arab State or Confederation of Arab States.

3. That in the brown area there shall be established an international administration, the form of which is to be decided upon after consultation with Russia, and subsequently in consultation with the other Allies, and the representatives of the sherif of Mecca. […]

10. The British and French Governments, as the protectors of the Arab State, shall agree that they will not themselves acquire and will not consent to a third Power acquiring territorial possessions in the Arabian peninsula, nor consent to a third Power installing a naval base either on the east coast, or on the islands, of the Red Sea. This, however, shall not prevent such adjustment of the Aden frontier as may be necessary in consequence of recent Turkish aggression.

Walter Laqueur and Barry Rubin (eds.), The Israel-Arab Reader (New York: Penguin 2008), pp. 13–16.

detriment: disadvantage
to abdicate: to give up, to renounce
entailed: involved
suzerainty: political control over a partly autonomous state

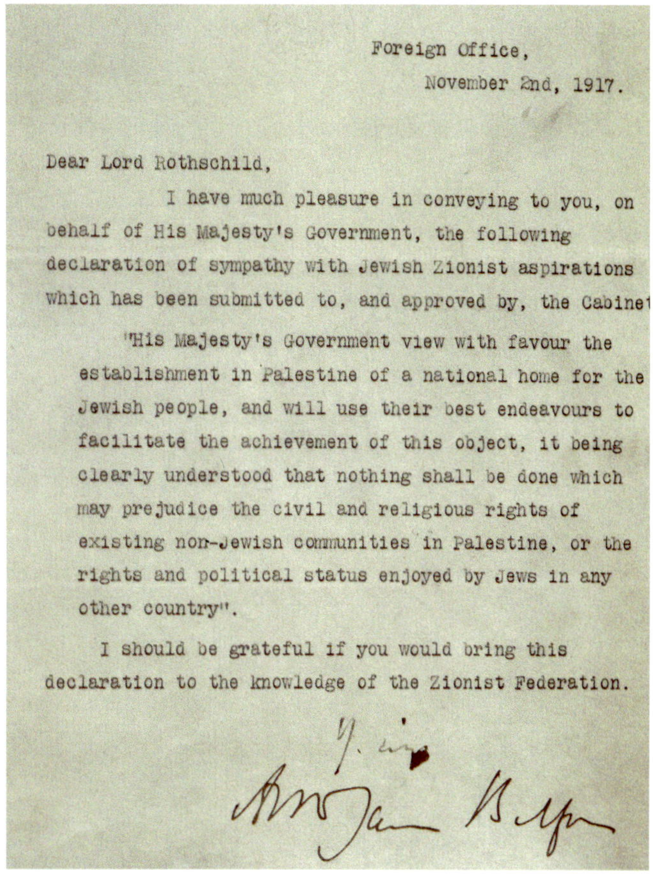

Foreign Office,
November 2nd, 1917.

Dear Lord Rothschild,

I have much pleasure in conveying to you, on behalf of His Majesty's Government, the following declaration of sympathy with Jewish Zionist aspirations which has been submitted to, and approved by, the Cabinet

"His Majesty's Government view with favour the establishment in Palestine of a national home for the Jewish people, and will use their best endeavours to facilitate the achievement of this object, it being clearly understood that nothing shall be done which may prejudice the civil and religious rights of existing non-Jewish communities in Palestine, or the rights and political status enjoyed by Jews in any other country".

I should be grateful if you would bring this declaration to the knowledge of the Zionist Federation.

M 11 The Balfour Declaration
Facsimile, 2 November 1917

Tasks

1. Write an answer to McMahon's letter, from the point of view of Hussein Ibn Ali, sherif of Mecca (M9).
2. List the most important provisions of the Sykes-Picot Agreement (M10).
3. Choose a task (text, M11):
   a) Portray the historical context of the Balfour Declaration.
   b) Find out more about the declaration's addressee, Lord Rothschild, and its author, James Balfour, on the Internet.
   c) Determine how binding the declaration was.
4. "Promises were made and commitments signed to satisfy all sides – though in spirit the documents were incompatible". Assess Schlicht's argument (text, p. 7).

The Holocaust (Shoah) and the Founding of Israel

National Socialism and Palestine

In the same year when World War II and the worst genocide in history began, the British White Paper suggested that immigration to Palestine be restricted. The plan could not have been more historically inappropriate

At the time, of course, nobody could have foreseen the dimensions of the "Shoah". However, it was evident to Jews that only a national home could provide a safe haven for those escaping from Nazi persecution as it moved from European country to country. In fact, the majority of Jews killed by the Nazis were not Germans, but Jews from other European countries under German occupation. Between 1933 and 1939 around 150,000 Jews had already left Germany, not all of whom went to Palestine. For the British, unlimited immigration to Palestine meant a deteriorating situation and a disruptive military challenge exactly when World War II required their complete attention.

Arabs saw a threat to their political ambitions and the founding of an Arab state in the increasing number of Jews in Palestine. The developments in Europe made a Jewish state seem inevitable and urgent. The USA especially favoured the goal as stated in the Biltmore Programme in New York in 1942. The more Jews insisted on founding a state in Palestine, the stronger Palestinian nationalism and the will to establish an Arab-Palestinian state became. As the expected "Arab empire" was not founded after World War I, Pan-Arab nationalism was no longer realistic, so Arabs had to identify with their respective country or region. This helped shape nationalism and political awareness among Palestinian Arabs. Support for a Palestinian-Arab state was hard to find. Arabs regarded the British more and more as their enemies.

One incidence of cooperation in these years has become notorious. The Grand Mufti of Jerusalem entered into an alliance with Nazi Germany. The Germans, enemies of the Jews, agreed to support the Arab cause. In case of a German victory the Arabs were promised their own state, full independence and control over all of Palestine. The Mufti went to Europe, where he was used by the Nazis in their efforts to gain Muslim support. It would be unjust to conclude that Palestinians in general supported the Nazis, German racial discrimination or Nazi genocide. When the Arab League was founded in 1945, regret of Jewish persecution at the hands of European dictators was expressed, but Arabs insisted that they should not be forced to pay for crimes committed by Europeans.

M 1

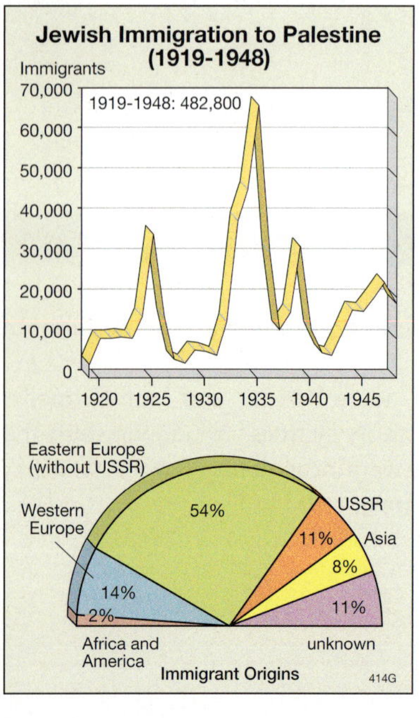

Founding the State of Israel

Meanwhile demographic realities in Palestine had changed considerably: The population had risen from 816,000 in 1922 to 1.94 million in 1946. In 1922 nearly 84,000 Jews lived in Palestine, but by 1946 there were 600,000 (nearly a third of the population). During the Second World War the most massive genocide in human history took place in Europe. The majority of European Jews – six million human beings – were annihilated in German extermination camps according to premeditated plans. Details of atrocities and the scope of the genocide became clear only after the end of the war. They made the

M 2 **Founding the State of Israel in Tel Aviv**
The future Prime Minister David Ben Gurion reads out the Proclamation of Independence on 14 May 1948, addressing the representatives of all parties.

M 3

founding of a Jewish state an undisputed goal among western powers. As terror and civil war in Palestine continued, the British, facing a severe economic crisis, decided to dispose of a problem which they could no longer control.

In 1947 Britain terminated its Mandate for Palestine. The newly founded United Nations was put in charge of the territory. The UN at first considered one binational state but in the face of stout resistance from both sides made plans for two states in Palestine: one Jewish, one Arab. The Jewish state already had provisional governmental structures in place. When the British left the country on 14 May 1948, the state of Israel was founded.

A large number of Arab refugees fled from the territory under Jewish control. Thus, a genuinely Jewish state could be founded. The attack of Palestine's neighbouring Arab states on Israel failed. Palestinians called the outcome of the first Arab-Israeli war "Naqba" – catastrophe. The "War of Independence" left Israel in possession of most of the territory of Palestine – much more than the UN plan had foreseen. The only state was a Jewish state. A Palestinian state was never founded.

The remaining territories of Palestine came under the control of Jordan (the West Bank, i.e., the area west of the Jordan River, including East Jerusalem) and Egypt (the Gaza Strip). There seemed to be neither territory for nor interest in a Palestinian state. By the end of 1948 about 700,000 Arabs had fled from territories under Jewish control; at the end of the War of Independence about 716,000 Jews and 92,000 Arabs lived in Israel. Large numbers of Palestinian refugees lived in camps in neighbouring Arab countries. They were secondary victims of the Holocaust – "victims of the victims".

In Israel a new "Jewish nation" developed. Russian Jews and French Jews had very little in common and difficulty communicating with each other. Even Herzl could not have expected these problems to be overcome. But Israel succeeded in modernizing Hebrew (a sacred language similar to Latin for nearly 2000 years) and made it the official language of the state. Hebrew today is a modern language and the national basis of communication, a bond uniting Jews from all over the world. Israel has also had a considerable number of inhabitants with Arabic as their mother tongue since its founding.

Founding the State of Israel

M 4 "Palestine"
Cartoon by Fritz Behrendt

M 5 Proclamation of Independence

The Proclamation of Independence was published by the Provisional State Council in Tel Aviv on 14 May 1948. The Provisional State Council was the forerunner of the Knesset, the Israeli parliament. The British Mandate was terminated the following day and regular armed forces of Transjordan, Egypt, Syria and other Arab countries entered Palestine.

The Land of Israel was the birthplace of the Jewish people. Here their spiritual, religious and national identity was formed. Here they achieved independence and created a culture of national and universal significance. Here they wrote and gave the Bible to the world.

Exiled from the Land of Israel the Jewish people remained faithful to it in all the countries of their *dispersion*, never ceasing to pray and hope for their return and the restoration of their national freedom.

Impelled by this historic association, Jews strove throughout the centuries to go back to the land of their fathers and regain their statehood. In recent decades they returned in their masses. They reclaimed the wilderness, revived their language, built cities and villages, and established a vigorous and ever-growing community, with its own economic and cultural life. They sought peace, yet were prepared to defend themselves. They brought the blessings of progress to all inhabitants of the country and looked forward to sovereign independence.

In the year 1897 the First Zionist Congress, inspired by Theodor Herzl's vision of the Jewish State, proclaimed the right of the Jewish people to national revival in their own country.

This right was acknowledged by the Balfour Declaration of November 2, 1917, and re-affirmed by the Mandate of the League of Nations, which gave explicit international recognition to the historic connection of the Jewish people with Palestine and their right to reconstitute their National Home.

The recent holocaust, which engulfed millions of Jews in Europe, proved anew the need to solve the problem of the homelessness and lack of independence of the Jewish people by means of the re-establishment of the Jewish State, which would open the gates to all Jews and *endow* the Jewish people with equality of status among the family of nations.

The survivors of the disastrous slaughter in Europe, and also Jews from other lands, have not *desisted* from their efforts to reach Eretz-Yisrael, in face of difficulties, obstacles and perils; and have not ceased to urge their right to a life of dignity, freedom and honest *toil* in their ancestral land.

In the Second World War the Jewish people in Palestine made their full contribution to the struggle of the freedom-loving nations against the Nazi evil. The sacrifices of their soldiers and their war effort gained them the right to rank with the nations which founded the United Nations.

On November 29, 1947, the General Assembly of the United Nations adopted a Resolution requiring the establishment of a Jewish State in Palestine. The General Assembly called upon the inhabitants of the country to take all the necessary steps on their part to put the plan into effect. This recognition by the United Nations of the right of the Jewish people to establish their independent State is *unassailable*.

It is the natural right of the Jewish people to lead, as do all other nations, an independent existence in its sovereign State.

Accordingly we, the members of the National Council, representing the Jewish people in Palestine and the World Zionist Movement, are met together in solemn assembly today, the day of termination of the British Mandate for Palestine; and by virtue of the natural and historic right of the Jewish people and of the Resolution of the General Assembly of the United Nations.

We hereby proclaim the establishment of the Jewish State in Palestine, to be called Medinath Yisrael (The State of Israel).

We hereby declare that, as from the termination of the Mandate at midnight, the 14th–15th May, 1948, and *pending* the setting up of the duly elected bodies of the State in accordance with a Constitution, to be drawn up by the Constituent Assembly not later than the 1st October, 1948, the National Council shall act as the Provisional State Council, and that the National Administration shall constitute the Provisional Government of the Jewish State, which shall be known as Israel.

The state of Israel will be open to the immigration of Jews from all countries of their dispersion; will promote the development of the country for the benefit of all its inhabitants; will be based on the principles of liberty, justice and peace as conceived by the Prophets of Israel; will uphold the full social and political equality of all its citizens, without distinction of religion, race, or sex; will guarantee freedom of religion, conscience, education and culture; will safeguard the Holy Places of all religions; and will loyally uphold the principles of the United Nations Charter.

The state of Israel will be ready to co-operate with the organs and representatives of the United Nations in the implementation of the Resolution of the Assembly of November 29, 1947, and will take steps to bring about the Economic Union over the whole of Palestine.

We appeal to the United Nations to assist the Jewish people in the building of its State and to admit Israel into the family of nations.

In the midst of *wanton* aggression, we yet call upon the Arab inhabitants of the State of Israel to preserve the ways of peace and play their part in the development of the State, on the basis of full and equal citizenship and due representation in all its bodies and institutions – provisional and permanent.

We extend our hand in peace and neighbourliness to all the neighbouring states and their peoples, and invite them to co-operate with the independent Jewish nation for the common good of all. The State of Israel is prepared to make its contribution to the progress of the Middle East as a whole.

Our call goes out to the Jewish people all over the world to rally to our side in the task of immigration and development, and to stand by us in the great struggle for the fulfillment of the dream of generations for the redemption of Israel.

With trust in the Rock of Israel, we set our hand to this Declaration, at this Session of the Provisional State Council, on the soil of the Homeland, in the city of Tel-Aviv [...]

Walter Laqueur and Barry Rubin (eds.), The Israel-Arab Reader (New York: Penguin 2008), pp. 81–83.

to disperse: to spread in different directions
to endow: to provide with
to desist: to stop doing sth.
toil: difficult and tiring work
unassailable: impossible to defeat, criticize
pending: while waiting for
wanton: having no just cause

Tasks

1. Analyse the cartoon (M4).
2. Assess the main information (text, M1, M4) on
   a) the needs and wishes of the Israelis and Palestinians,
   b) demographic changes in the Middle East between 1922 and 1946,
   c) the role of Germany and the United Nations.
3. Evaluate the "Proclamation of Independence" (M5) in its historical context.

A Story of Wars 1948–2010

M 1 Battle in Jaffa 1948
Palestinians fight against Jewish military forces shortly after the founding of Israel, 1948

War of Independence 1948

The state of Israel was born during a war in which all its neighbours opposed its sheer existence.

Arabs denied Jews who had immigrated to Palestine the right to found a state in what Arabs considered "their" country. However, after the traumatic experience of the Holocaust Jews felt a desperate need for a country of their own to serve as a safe haven – a Jewish state with no discrimination and no danger of annihilation. The long-standing conflict between the Arabs and Israel is based on these two mutually exclusive points of view. After the war of independence the chance to achieve peace or a general solution of the conflict was lost.

The "Naqba" or catastrophe, as the founding of Israel was called in the Arab world, shocked the whole Arab nation. It led to revolutions *toppling* traditional governments in Egypt, Syria, and other countries where new movements replaced corrupt regimes which had failed to prevent the establishment of the state of Israel. Popular reformist parties favouring Pan-Arabism and Arab socialism assumed political control first in Cairo, then in Damascus, and later in Baghdad. They were opposed to Israel (together with her allies) and to imperialism in the Middle East in general. Israel, on the other hand, did little to reconcile her Arab neighbours.

to topple: to make sth. fall
tenet: principle or belief
asset: a major benefit

During the Cold War

The conflict fit into the global divisions emerging after World War II. The Soviet Union – after having originally favoured the founding of the Jewish state – soon threw in her lot with the Arabs in their fight against a state sponsored by imperialism. The "West" (Great Britain, France and the USA), on the other hand, backed Israel. Thus, the Middle East conflict became part of the broader context of the East-West conflict with its global dimensions and inherent risk of large-scale hostilities involving the superpowers.

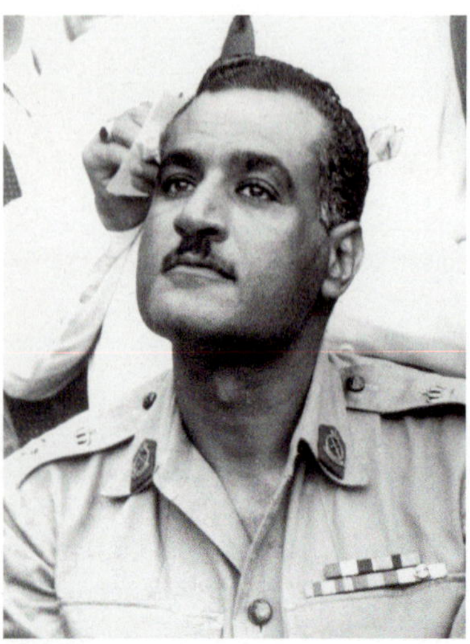

M 2 Gamal Abdel Nasser (1918–1970)
Photograph, February 1954

The Suez Crisis 1956

In Egypt a young, charismatic officer who had participated in the 1948 war rose to prominence after the revolution of 1952: Gamal Abdel-Nasser became the undisputed leader of Egypt and soon attained the status of a popular hero throughout the entire Arab world. As a prominent representative of the non-aligned movement Nasser assumed a leading position globally. While Nasser's *tenets* of Arab unity, the Palestinian cause, anti-imperialism and non-alignment made him an idol of the Arab masses and an *asset* for the Soviet Union in the Middle East, he automatically became an enemy of Israel, France and Britain – especially as he didn't shy away from conflict. On the contrary, by his very emphatic language and actions Nasser raised tensions. Relations with European powers still present in the Middle East deteriorated, reaching a low point in 1956. In 1955 Egypt had already blockaded the Gulf of Aqaba, sealing off the Israeli port. On 26 July (1956) Nasser held an emotional speech severely criticizing Israel and the Western powers. He also nationalized the Suez Canal, which still was under Anglo-French control. This offered Great Britain, France and Israel the opportunity to intervene: In a coordinated military operation they attacked Egypt. Israel advanced, occupying the Gaza Strip and the Sinai to the Suez Canal, whereas British and French airborne troops invaded the Canal Zone and bombed Egyptian cities. The USSR threatened to intervene. The USA, fearing the growth of Soviet influence in the Middle East as a consequence of the attack on Egypt, called for the aggressors to withdraw. What had looked like a military catastrophe for Egypt resulted in a tremendous success for Nasser as British, French and Israeli troops retreated. Egypt emerged stronger than ever. Nasser's regime was not defeated, but consolidated.

M 3 Israeli Soldiers at the Western ("Wailing") Wall
After taking East Jerusalem during the Six-Day War, 1967

The Six-Day War 1967

Relations in the Middle East remained tense. Nasser continued to use the Palestine problem to raise emotional support in the region. In the mid-sixties Nasser asked that UN troops stationed in Sinai leave and once again closed the Gulf of Aqaba to Israel. Verbal attacks on Israel intensified and military cooperation among Arab partners was planned. In this situation Israel worried about an imminent Arab attack. An Israeli pre-emptive strike against the neighbouring Arab states on 5 June (1967) *forestalled* any Arab military action and destroyed Arab aircraft on the ground. Israeli troops advanced, occupying the Gaza Strip (Egyptian), the West Bank and East Jerusalem (Jordanian), as well as the Golan Heights (Syrian). Israel had weakened its opponents considerably and extended its territory. Notwithstanding international and UN pressure, Israel kept the newly conquered territories, returning only the Sinai in a separate peace with Egypt. All the other territories occupied in 1967 are still under Israeli control.

to forestall: to prevent

This time military failure also meant defeat for President Nasser. "Nasserism" never recovered from the Six-Day War; its popular support and historic momentum were lost. Nasser and his ideology of Arab socialism had not brought about the change and success which many Arabs, not only Egyptians, had expected.

M 4 Palestinian Refugee Camp near Amman
The Six-Day War led to a new wave of Palestinian refugees: 500,000 people left regions occupied by Israel and fled to neighbouring Arab countries, Photograph, 1969.

The Yom Kippur/Ramadan War 1973

President Nasser died unexpectedly in 1970. His successor, Vice-President Anwar as-Sadat, took office at a time of historic change in the Middle East conflict. Sadat realized that "Nasserism" had died before Nasser and that new concepts were needed, because his predecessors had offered no solution to the conflict. He would try a completely new approach. First of all, however, to achieve success with his plans, he had to restore Arab honour.

This meant that he had to overcome the humiliating defeat of 1967. In 1973 during Ramadan and on the Jewish high holiday of Yom Kippur (Day of *Atonement*), he and his ally Syria launched a surprise attack on Israel on the Suez front. The Egyptians overran Israeli positions, the prestigious Bar-Lev Line and penetrated deep into Sinai. On the Golan front a similar Syrian operation started at the same time. However, Egyptian troops did not take full advantage of their position – as if not prepared for their swift success.

atonement: repentance, remorse

M 5 The Yom Kippur War
Israeli soldiers during the Yom Kippur War in Sinai with Egyptian prisoners under Egyptian artillery fire, 1973

Israel recovered within several days and led a counterstrike. Even though Israeli troops crossed the Suez Canal and only withdrew from Egyptian territory under pressure from the US, Sadat's initial success had been enough to restore Egyptian self-confidence and pride. He now felt ready for his original goal: To negotiate the end of the conflict with Israel. This made him a traitor to the common cause in the eyes of many Arabs, but in many parts of the world Sadat was seen as a hero of peace. With the Camp David negotiations in the 1970s the hostilities between Israel and Egypt finally came to an end.

Israel in Lebanon 1982 and 2006

This was far from an end to the Middle East conflict. The Palestinians – those who were, in fact, most affected by the founding of Israel – moved into the focus of the conflict increasingly as independent players. Through spectacular international acts of terror they succeeded in attracting attention worldwide.

M 6 **Massacre in Sabra and Shatila in Lebanon, 1982**
Arab-Christian-Lebanese militias massacred Palestinian refugees in the Camps of Sabra and Shatila, killing between 2,000 and 3,000 people.
Photograph, September 18, 1982

At first Jordan, then Lebanon, served as a base of their operations against Israel. Thus, a new pattern of conflict developed: There were no more traditional wars between the Israeli army and the armies of Arab states. Instead, Arab guerrillas operating in neighbouring countries provoked Israeli military actions. For example, the invasion of Lebanon in 1982 was meant to dislodge the PLO and its allies from their positions, to destroy their military potential, and to weaken Syria's role in Lebanon.

Another Israeli operation against Lebanon in summer 2006 struck at Hezbollah, a Lebanese Shiite group receiving support from Syria and Iran. This operation was preceded by years of conflict over the border between Lebanon and Syria, Hezbollah frequently launching rocket attacks against targets on Israeli territory.

The Gaza Strip and the West Bank

Recently, Israel has repeatedly attacked autonomous territories in the West Bank and the Gaza Strip because, according to Israel, attacks were planned, organized or carried out from these areas while Palestinian authorities did not do enough to prevent such operations.

A special situation arose in Gaza after the Israelis withdrew from the area. Hamas took over control in Gaza, but Fatah had control of the Palestinian territories in the West Bank. Hamas took a more radical stand against Israel than Fatah (now considered moderate) and used its position in the Gaza Strip to launch rocket attacks into Israel. Tensions between the Hamas regime in the Gaza Strip and Israel have grown considerably since 2006. Towards the end of December 2008 Israel started Operation "Cast Lead", one of the recent major military actions to destroy or to weaken Hamas, resulting in the loss of civilian lives, the destruction of infrastructure and deterioration of living conditions in Gaza. Small-scale warfare is part of daily life in Israeli-Palestinian relations.

The Situation after the East-West Conflict

The international context of the conflict has changed considerably in the last decades. With the fall of the Communist bloc, the diminished role of Russia and the collapse of a bipolar world order, only one superpower, the USA, remained to exert real influence or pressure on both parties. The USA found herself in a position where she had to manage the conflict, control both sides to a certain extent, and initiate efforts for peace. The USA had to mobilize Arab support (for example, in the Iraq wars) to consolidate her influence in the Middle East. She was thus obliged to take a more balanced position in the Middle East conflict, rather than offering one-sided support to Israel alone.

A Story of Wars – Analysing Points of View

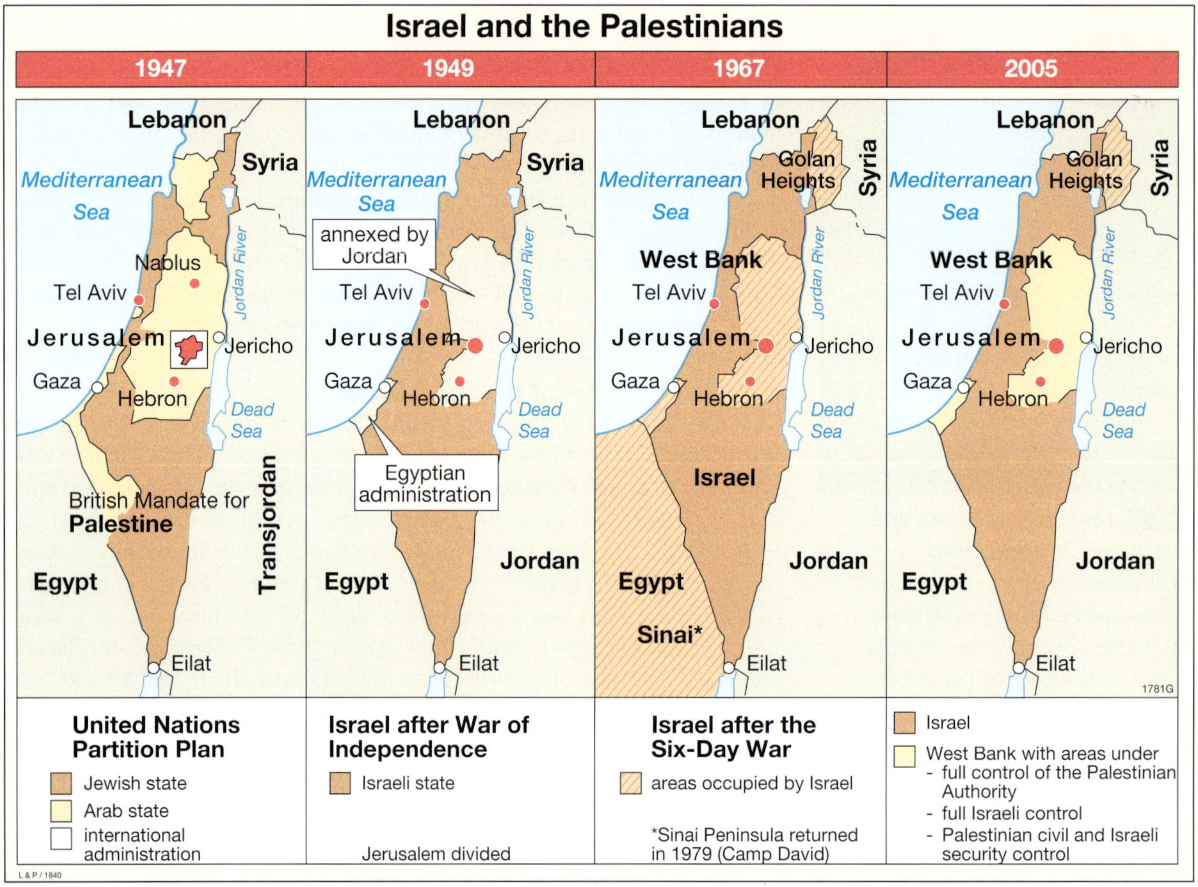

M 7

M 8 The Six-Day War

a) Egyptian President Gamal Abdel Nasser, Speech to National Assembly Members (29 May 1967):

[…] Brothers, the revolt, upheaval and *commotion* which we now see taking place in every Arab country are not only because we have returned to the Gulf of Aqabah or rid ourselves of the *UNEF*, but because we have restored Arab honour and renewed Arab hopes.

Israel used to boast a great deal, and the Western powers, headed by the United States and Britain, used to ignore and even despise us and consider us of no value. But now that the time has come – and I have already said in the past that we will decide the time and place and not allow them to decide – we must be ready for triumph and not for a recurrence of the 1948 comedies. We shall triumph, God willing.

Preparations have already been made. We are now ready to confront Israel. They have claimed many things about the 1956 Suez war, but no one believed them after the secrets of the 1956 *collusion* were uncovered – that mean collusion in which Israel took part. Now we are ready for the confrontation. We are now ready to deal with the entire Palestine question.

The issue now at hand is not the Gulf of Aqabah, the Straits of Tiran, or the withdrawal of the UNEF, but the rights of the Palestine people. It is the aggression which took place in Palestine in 1948 with the collaboration of Britain and the United States. It is the expulsion of the Arabs from Palestine, the usurpation of their rights, and the plunder of their property. It is the *disavowal* of all the UN resolutions in favour of the Palestinian people.

The issue today is far more serious than they say. They want *to confine* the issue to the Straits of Tiran, the UNEF and the right of passage. We demand the full rights of the Palestinian people. We say this out of our belief that Arab rights cannot be *squandered* because the Arabs throughout the Arab world are demanding these Arab rights.

We are not afraid of the United States and its threats, of Britain and her threats, or of the entire Western world and its partiality to Israel. The United States and Britain are partial to Israel and give no consideration to the Arabs, to the entire Arab nation. Why? Because we have made them believe that we cannot distinguish between friend and foe. We must make them know that we know who our foes are and who our friends are and treat them accordingly.

If the United States and Britain are partial to Israel, we must say that our enemy is not only Israel but also the United States and Britain and treat them as such. If the Western Powers disavow our rights and ridicule and despise us, we Arabs must teach them to respect us and take us seriously. Otherwise all our talk about Palestine, the Palestinian people, and Palestinian rights will be null and void and of no consequence. We must treat enemies as enemies and friends as friends.

Walter Laqueur and Barry Rubin (eds.), The Israel-Arab Reader (New York: Penguin 2008), pp. 102–103.

b) UN Security Council, Resolution 242:

November 22, 1967

The Security Council,

Expressing its continuing concern with the grave situation in the Middle East,

Emphasizing the *inadmissibility* of the acquisition of territory by war and the need to work for a just and lasting peace in which every state in the area can live in security.

Emphasizing further that all member states in their acceptance of the Charter of the United Nations have undertaken a commitment to act in accordance with Article 2 of the Charter,

1. Affirms that the fulfillment of Charter principles requires the establishment of a just and lasting peace in the Middle East which should include the application of both the following principles:

(i) Withdrawal of Israeli armed forces from territories occupied in the recent conflict;

(ii) Termination of all claims or states of *belligerency* and respect for and acknowledgment of the sovereignty, territorial integrity and political independence of every state in the area and their right to live in peace within secure and recognized boundaries free from threats or acts of force;

2. Affirms further the necessity

(a) For guaranteeing freedom of navigation through international waterways in the area;

(b) For achieving a just settlement of the refugee problem;

(c) For guaranteeing the territorial inviolability and political independence of every state in the area, through measures including the establishment of demilitarized zones;

3. Requests the Secretary General to designate a special representative to proceed to the Middle East to establish and maintain contacts with the states concerned in order to promote agreement and assist efforts to achieve a peaceful and accepted settlement in accordance with the provisions and principles in this resolution.

4. Requests the Secretary General to report to the Security Council on the progress of the efforts of the special representative as soon as possible.

Walter Laqueur and Barry Rubin (eds.), The Israel-Arab Reader (New York: Penguin 2008), p. 116.

M 9 Position of the Soviet Union

A letter from the Secretary General of the CPSU, Leonid Brezhnev, to the Algerian President Boumedienne explains the Soviet position on the War of 1973 (9 October 1973):

The responsibility for the new military flare-up in the Middle East lies wholly and completely with the Tel Aviv leaders. While enjoying the support and protection of imperialist circles, Israel continues its aggression started in 1967 against the Arab countries, and *foils* every effort to establish a just peace in the Middle East and deliberately carries out provocations, including armed provocations, against Syria, Egypt and Lebanon, thus aggravating to the extreme the situation in this region.

I believe, dear comrade President, you agree that (in) the struggle at present being waged against

commotion: excited, confused activity
UNEF: United Nations Emergency Force
collusion: secret agreement with the intention of cheating or deceiving
to disavow: to deny, not to acknowledge
to confine: to keep within limits
to squander: to waste
inadmissibility: sth. that cannot be allowed
belligerency: aggression, waging war
to foil: to prevent sb. from doing sth.

Israeli aggression, for the liberation of Arab territories occupied in 1967 and the safeguarding of the legitimate rights of the Arab people of Palestine, Arab fraternal solidarity must, more than ever before, play a decisive role. Syria and Egypt must not be alone in their struggle against a treacherous enemy. There is an urgent need for the widest aid and support of the progressive regimes in these countries who, like Algeria, are the hope for progress and freedom in the Arab world.

The Central Committee of the CPSU and the Soviet Government are firmly convinced that the Algerian leaders, who are widely experienced in the anti-imperialist struggle, understand full well all the peculiarities of the present situation and that, guided by the ideals of fraternal solidarity, will use every means and take every step required to give their support to Syria and Egypt in the tough struggle imposed by the Israeli aggressor.

Walter Laqueur and Barry Rubin (eds.), The Israel-Arab Reader (New York: Penguin 2008).

M 10 European Council

Declaration on the Middle East by the European Council issued at the conclusion of a two-day conference in Venice (13 June 1980):

The Heads of State or Government and the Ministers of Foreign Affairs [...] agreed that growing tensions affecting this region constitute a serious danger and render a comprehensive solution to the Israeli-Arab conflict more necessary and pressing than ever. [...]

[T]he time has come to promote the recognition and implementation of the two principles universally accepted by the international community: the right to existence and to security of all the States in the region, including Israel, and justice for all the peoples, which implies the recognition of the legitimate rights of the Palestinian people.

All of the countries in the area are entitled to live in peace within secure, recognized and guaranteed borders. The necessary guarantees for a peace settlement should be provided by the United Nations by a decision of the Security Council and, if necessary, on the basis of other mutually agreed procedures. The Nine [member states of the European Community] declare that they are prepared to participate within the framework of a comprehensive settlement in a system of concrete and binding international guarantees, including guarantees on the ground.

A just solution must finally be found to the Palestinian problem, which is not simply one of refugees. The Palestinian people, which is conscious of existing as such, must be placed in a position, by an appropriate process defined within the framework of the comprehensive peace settlement, to exercise fully its right to self-determination

Walter Laqueur and Barry Rubin (eds.), The Israel-Arab Reader (New York: Penguin 2008), p. 232–233.

Tasks

1. Work on a photograph of your choice (M1, M3, M4, M5, M6):
   a) Describe your first impression. Point out what attracts your interest. Note what confuses you.
   b) Describe the scene that is photographed.
   c) Depict the situation in which the photograph played a role.
   d) Determine who is addressed by the photograph.
   e) Assess the effect the photograph had and will continue to have.
2. Characterize Gamal Abdel Nasser and sum up his 1967 speech in your own words (M2, M8).
3. Describe the main territorial changes in Palestine after the founding of Israel and explain how these changes came about (M7).
4. Summarize the central arguments of the UN Security Council Resolution and debate in groups (in class, with classmates) whether the resolution is more in favour of Israel or Palestine.
5. a) Assess the possible motives behind the position of the USSR (M9).
   b) State your personal opinion of the Soviet position.
6. Evaluate the Venice Declaration in its historical context (M10).

Crossroads to Peace – Is there a Palestinian Nation?

Peace between Israel and Egypt: Camp David

In 2009 US President Obama received the Nobel Peace Prize in recognition of his efforts to revive the exhausted Middle East peace process and for expressing his determination to pursue a lasting peace in the near century-long conflict between Israel and the Palestinians. From the founding of Israel in 1948 to the Israeli-Egyptian peace treaty in the 1970s, war and conflict dominated the Middle Eastern scene. Egypt's President Sadat paved the way for a bilateral peace by visiting Israel, a move no Arab head of state would have even considered previously. Thereafter, it made sense for those primarily affected by the conflict to also seek peace. If Egypt and Israel could find a way of settling their disputes and diverging interests, why couldn't Palestinians and Israelis follow this example?

In the Camp David Accords of 1978 Egypt, Israel and the USA planned a kind of autonomy for the Palestinians. All of Palestine was under Israeli control at the time; Palestinian autonomy was meant to be the first step towards a comprehensive peace. However, further steps were not taken for years. Mutual distrust, hatred and lack of courage to compromise or give up traditional demands were too deeply rooted on both sides.

M 1 Camp David
Menachim Begin, Jimmy Carter and Anwar as-Sadat
Photograph, September 1978

M 2 **Yassir Arafat (1929–2004)**
Photograph, about 2000

Peace for the Palestinians, Too?

At the beginning of the twentieth century a vague Arab nationalism never found its expression in statehood. An Arab empire, a national state for Arabs, was never founded. Palestinian national identity emerged during the second quarter of the century in the conflicts with the British Mandate and Jewish groups. In the first decades of Israel's existence, Palestinian national consciousness arose as dissatisfaction with the ineffective support of the Arab states for the Palestinian cause grew. Palestinians organized themselves, formulated their political goals and insisted on a state of their own. The USA as well as the EU gradually recognized that the Palestinian problem concerned not only refugees but also the Palestinian people's right of self-determination. At first both sides were incapable of entering into bilateral negotiations, because the Palestinians refused to accept Israel's right of existence, while Israel refused to recognize the Palestinian Liberation Organization (PLO) as official representatives of the Palestinian people. Although the Camp David Accords of 1978 established general guidelines, decisive steps towards a real peace took much longer. A semi-private initiative of Norwegian personalities led to a secret meeting in Oslo, where Israelis and PLO representatives assembled around one table, negotiating as partners for the very first time. This was the essential breakthrough which made "Oslo" unique.

When Palestinians recognized the existence of the state of Israel and Israel recognized the PLO as the legal representatives of the Palestinian people, the foundation for discussing peace and coexistence in one and the same country was laid.

"Land for Peace": The Oslo Process

"Land for peace" seemed to be the formula which could bring about a peaceful settlement of the Middle East conflict. In the Oslo Process both sides agreed that Israel would withdraw from territories in the West Bank and Gaza occupied in 1967. Also, a Palestinian National Authority (PNA) would assume control of the territories evacuated by Israeli troops. In this way the Palestinians would attain autonomy to a certain extent. Palestinian free and general elections would be held.

M 3 **Gaza-Jericho Agreement**
Rabin, Clinton and Arafat
Photograph, 1994

M 4 **"The Leopard Changes his Spots"**
Cartoon by Karl-Heinz Schoenfeld, 1993

After an interim period a subsequent agreement would deal with the founding of an independent Palestinian state, the status of Jerusalem, Palestinian refugees and Jewish settlements on Palestinian territory. The agreement (Oslo I) was signed in Washington in 1993.
An immediate effect of Oslo was the end of the Palestinian popular uprising, the "Intifada", which had erupted in 1987 out of Palestinian frustration, lack of perspective, deteriorating political and economic conditions, and violence. Oslo sparked optimism and the vision of a brighter future. A solution to the Middle East conflict seemed realistic. In 1995 a further accord, the Interim Agreement on the West Bank and the Gaza Strip (Oslo II), set out details for the Israeli military withdrawal from cities, towns and villages.

The Palestinian territories were divided into "Zone A" under Palestinian administration, "Zone B" under civilian responsibility of the PNA but under Israeli security control, and "Zone C" (nearly 60% of the territories) under full Israeli control.

From the beginning the Oslo Process and the resulting concessions met with severe criticism from both sides. Later political developments created a climate which made further progress towards peace impossible, as Israeli right-wing governments come to power and the more radical Islamic movement Hamas gained influence among Palestinians. Violence and difficulties in daily life increased. Both Palestinians and Israelis lost confidence in a successful peace process.

M 5 **The Palestinian Territories before the Evacuation of the Settlements in the Gaza Strip (2004)**

The "Middle East Quartet"

The USA, lacking Arab support for her Middle East policies, tried to revive the peace process on an international level. In 2002 a "Quartet on the Middle East", consisting of the USA, the UN, the EU and Russia, arranged to negotiate a road map towards a solution of the Middle East conflict by 2005. The Quartet's goal of founding a Palestinian state proved to be unrealistic, although even radical Palestinian groups participated in the short armistices which became effective. In 2006 Hamas emerged from elections as the strongest political force among Palestinians. Both the USA and Israel refused to negotiate with the group as long as it did not renounce violence. Israeli military action in Gaza and Lebanon increased tensions. Furthermore, the Israeli newspaper Haaretz published secret information that settlements in the occupied territories were being extended, in violation of Israeli obligations. The road map to peace seemed doomed.

In 2009 elections in Israel led to a right-wing coalition under Prime Minister Netanyahu. Under pressure from US President Obama, Netanyahu declared his acceptance of a Palestinian state for the first time, although he noted many reservations, including demilitarization, the exclusion of Jerusalem and ongoing settlement activities. It is not yet clear whether President Obama will be able to fulfil the hopes raised when he was awarded the Nobel Peace Prize in 2009. During US Vice President Biden's visit to Israel and the Palestinian territories in March 2010, Israel announced the construction of more new settlements in East Jerusalem, openly contradicting the American request not to build any new settlements on disputed territory. This met with severe criticism from all over the world, including even Jewish organizations. However, Prime Minister Netanyahu clearly depends on support from right-wing parties. The permanent major impediments to peace remain: Jewish settlements in Palestine, Jerusalem and Palestinian refugees. In addition, the scarcity of water resources and their distribution among Israelis and Palestinians will be of growing importance in the peace process. In March 2010 the Middle East Quartet met again in Moscow to resume its efforts toward peace.

"Peace Now"

A peace movement was formed in Israeli civil society in the late 1970s. "Peace Now" is the most prominent group, with the author Amos Oz an internationally recognized representative. The number of Israeli conscientious objectors has grown recently. They claim that the Israeli army has broken international law and attacked civilian targets.

M 6 "Peace is the Way" and "Stop the Occupation"
Israeli-Palestinian demonstration, Tel Aviv, 2002

The Camp David Accords (1978) – Analysing a diplomatic document

M 7 A Framework for Peace in the Middle East

This document was negotiated by Egyptian President Anwar as-Sadat, Israeli Prime Minister Menachem Begin and President Jimmy Carter at Camp David, in Thurmont, Maryland, then signed by Sadat and Begin and witnessed by Carter at the White House on 17 September 1978:

Preamble: The search for peace in the Middle East must be guided by the following:

- The agreed basis for a peaceful settlement of the conflict between Israel and its neighbors is United Nations Security Council Resolution 242, in all its parts.
- After four wars during thirty years, despite intensive human efforts, the Middle East, which is the cradle of civilization and the birthplace of three great religions, does not yet enjoy the blessings of peace. The people of the Middle East yearn for peace so that the vast human and natural resources of the region can be turned to the pursuits of peace and so that this area can become a model for coexistence and cooperation among nations.
- The historic initiative of President Sadat in visiting Jerusalem and the reception accorded to him by the Parliament, government and people of Israel, and the reciprocal visit of Prime Minister Begin to Ismailia, the peace proposals made by both leaders, as well as the warm reception of these missions by the people of both countries, have created an unprecedented opportunity for peace which must not be lost if this generation and future generations are to be spared the tragedies of war. [...]

A. West Bank and Gaza

1. Egypt, Israel, Jordan and the representatives of the Palestinian people should participate in negotiations on the resolution of the Palestinian problem in all its aspects. To achieve that objective, negotiations relating to the West Bank and Gaza should proceed in three stages:

a) Egypt and Israel agree that, in order to ensure a peaceful and orderly transfer of authority, and taking into account the security concerns of all the parties, there should be transitional arrangements for the West Bank and Gaza for a period not exceeding five years. In order to provide full autonomy to the inhabitants, under these arrangements the Israeli military government and its civilian administration will be withdrawn as soon as a self-governing authority has been freely elected by the inhabitants of these areas to replace the existing military government. [...]

b) Egypt, Israel, and Jordan will agree on the modalities for establishing the elected self-governing authority in the West Bank and Gaza. The delegations of Egypt and Jordan may include Palestinians from the West Bank and Gaza or other Palestinians as mutually agreed. The parties will negotiate an agreement which will define the powers and responsibilities of the self-governing authority to be exercised in the West Bank and Gaza. A withdrawal of Israeli armed forces will take place and there will be a redeployment of the remaining Israeli forces into specified security locations. [...]

c) When the self-governing authority (administrative council) in the West Bank and Gaza is established and inaugurated, the transitional period of five years will begin. As soon as possible, but not later than the third year after the beginning of the transitional period, negotiations will take place to determine the final status of the West Bank and Gaza and its relationship with its neighbors, and to conclude a peace treaty between Israel and Jordan by the end of the transitional period. [...]

B. Egypt-Israel

1. Egypt and Israel undertake not to resort to the threat or the use of force to settle disputes. Any disputes shall be settled by peaceful means in accordance with the provisions of Article 33 of the Charter of the United Nations.

2. In order to achieve peace between them, the parties agree to negotiate in good faith with a goal of concluding within three months from the signing of this Framework a peace treaty between them, while inviting the other parties to the conflict to proceed simultaneously to negotiate and conclude similar peace treaties with a view to achieving a comprehensive peace in the area. The Framework for the Conclusion of a Peace Treaty between Egypt and Israel will govern the peace negotiations between them. [...]

C. Associated Principles

1. Egypt and Israel state that principles and provisions described below should apply to peace treaties between Israel and each of its neighbors – Egypt, Jordan, Syria and Lebanon.

Walter Laqueur and Barry Rubin (eds.), The Israel-Arab Reader (New York: Penguin 2008), p. 222–237.

The Intifada – Analysing Texts and Photographs

M 8 Intifada

The Israeli author Amira Hass reports on the outbreak of the First Intifada in 1987:

In December rage finally washed over Gaza. In the first few days, it seemed the whole Strip was swept up in the protests and yet at the same time everyone felt caught unaware, as if they were watching from the sidelines, amazed by the strength of the eruption. On the second day, December 10, Marwan Kafarna, who then lived in Beit Hanun, was unable to reach his school in Jabalia as it was under *curfew*. Instead, most *UNRWA* teachers, including Kafarna, were sent to schools near their homes to fill in for colleagues trapped elsewhere by the curfews.

However, like Abu Husa and Zaqut, Kafarna made his way to the union building. Ignoring the curfew, the three made a tour of the Strip to see what was going on. Jabalia had not been calmed by the curfew; quite the contrary. "There were barricades, burning tires, and rocks everywhere. Most of the roads were blocked and people were streaming out of their homes to join in, to find out what was happening." The three met more formally, "to move the situation along," as Kafarna puts it, possibly on the third day of rioting. Mabhuh was absent – he had been arrested the day before while preparing leaflets for the Communist Party and was held for nine days. Other Communists had begun distributing leaflets in the name of "Nationalist Forces" and the rest of the organizations in the Strip were furious at their exclusion. Still, the Communist Party's lone action highlighted the need for coordinating the riots, and the central union committee, which had been operative for several months, was the obvious address.

Rigid control of the press and suppression of all political activity quickly made the one-page leaflet – cheaply produced underground and easily distributed on the streets – the Strip's popular form of mass communication. Leaflets giving instructions, declaring strikes, conveying news, and offering moral support became common; even though the authors remained anonymous and secret, people followed the instructions and received each new leaflet eagerly. The *hallmark* of the intifada, however, was that the leaflets were signed jointly by rival political organizations. However, the first to appear in the name of the Unified National Leadership was endorsed only by Fatah, the *PFLP*, and the *DFLP*; Mabhuh was in jail, so the Communist Party's *imprimatur* was missing.

All four men (and Ihab al-Ashqar, who joined the UNL soon after) light up when they remember those early days. Each one added something to the overall strategy. "Fatah decided not to use weapons," Abu Husa explained. "We started planning other ways to keep up the intense level of activity. We'd get our people, the Fatah supporters, out into the streets and then stand aside, move out of the picture. They were the ones who needed to act, not the usual *suspects*. Of course, a lot of people wanted to know why we hadn't shown our faces at the protests, but we were busy doing other things. We'd flee from the soldiers and make sure they saw us running into people's houses. Then they'd *toss* in some tear gas or come in, smash things, beat the family up. The idea was that there'd be someone wounded in every home – we wanted every Palestinian to be involved, to resist the soldiers, whether they were politically active or not. That way we made sure the whole Strip participated."

Tawfiq Abu Husa decided to concentrate his energies on Fatah and so brought Ashqar to the second UNL meeting to replace him. "Even before I introduced myself," said Ashqar, "I told them not to contact the PLO leaders abroad, not for anything. I gave them an ultimatum: 'If the people abroad interfere, I quit.' Tawfiq and I saw eye to eye on this. We'd come to the conclusion that whatever we managed to do here, they somehow *wrecked* over there." Kafarna could not have

curfew: a rule that forbids people to go outside at certain times
UNRWA: United Nations Relief and Works Agency
hallmark: characteristic feature or quality
PFLP: Popular Front for the Liberation of Palestine
DFLP: Democratic Front for the Liberation of Palestine
imprimatur: (here) approval
suspect: sb. believed to have committed a crime
to toss: to throw
to wreck: to destroy, severely damage
sop: sth. offered to gain favour
retroactive: (here) written after the events

agreed more – he too disliked receiving instructions from the Popular Front abroad. Mabhuh, however, had no need of the ultimatum; the Communists' base was local. The DFLP also maintained a strong, well-coordinated leadership in Gaza and the West Bank and so Zaqut felt empowered to make decisions and act freely.

As a *sop* to the organizational hierarchy, UNL members sometimes wrote *retroactive* reports on their actions, which were passed on to contact people in their respective movements. Abu Husa, however, stayed in daily contact with Arafat's deputy, Abu Jihad, in Tunis. In one memorable conversation, Abu Husa tried to explain the scope of the demonstrations. "We've never seen anything like it," he said. "It's ... it's," he stammered, searching for the right word. "It's an intifada."

Amira Hass, Drinking the Sea at Gaza. Days and Nights in a Land Under Siege. Translated by Elana Wesley and Maxine Kaufman-Lacusta (New York: Henry Holt and Company: 2000), pp. 41–43.

M 9 Arrest

Israeli soldiers arrest a Palestinian for throwing stones during the Intifada in Ramallah (West Bank), 1987

Tasks

1. Write a short biography either of Anwar as-Sadat or of Yassir Arafat. Use the Internet.
2. Leaders involved in the Israeli-Palestinian conflict confronted difficulties in their attempts to negotiate a peace treaty. Assess those faced by the subject you chose in assignment 1 above, Sadat or Arafat (text).
3. Evaluate whether a Palestinian nation exists, using all the material given.
4. Interpret the cartoon (M4). Comment on its accuracy and fairness, giving reasons for your opinion.
5. Criticism of Israel's attempts to block peaceful solutions of the conflict is growing. Explain how the "Peace Now" movement may weaken this criticism (M6). Find more information on the Internet. Discuss your results in groups.
6. Place the Camp David document into its historical context and evaluate its results (text, M7).
7. a) Sum up Amira Hass's description of the Intifada.
   b) Analyse her opinion of the Palestinian uprising, giving proof of your arguments from the text.
8. Compare the text and the photograph (M8, M9). Assess which has a greater effect on you.

The Intifada – Analysing a Photograph

M 10 "Icon of the Intifada"

Palestine and Lebanese pupils with the picture of al-Duri's tragic death, Beirut, 18 October 2000

M 11 A Comment

Comment on the photograph in the New York Times, 7 February 2005:

Since the start of the second Palestinian uprising more than four years ago, many children have died in the gunfire. But it is the *harrowing* image of a single terrified 12-year-old boy, shielded in his father's futile embrace, that possesses the iconic power of a battle flag.

Tunisia and Egypt have issued postage stamps of the Palestinian child, Mohammed al-Duri, crouching in a fetal position against his father under attack from a fusillade of bullets in September 2000. Egypt also named a street in his honor, and suicide bombers invoked Mohammed as a martyr in videotaped farewells.

In France, far from Gaza's street battles, the *indelible* scene is a picture worth a thousand arguments. Here, a debate *seethes* about whether the ghastly televised *footage* of Mohammed al-Duri was genuine, misinterpreted or – as one American academic put it – artfully staged *"Pallywood" theater*.

Battle photographs have long been potent media weapons, and some of the most memorable war pictures have provoked questions about authenticity [...].

At the center of the dispute is state-run France 2 and its Jerusalem correspondent, Charles Enderlin, a veteran reporter who says fierce criticism about the channel's exclusive footage of the boy has provoked death threats against him. [...]

[A] 2002 German documentary called "Three Bullets and a Child: Who Killed the Young Mohammed al-Duri?" tried to address *lingering* questions about whether the child was killed by Israelis or Palestinians.

Last week, the issue gained fresh momentum after a prominent French editor and an independent television producer broke ranks in the country's media circles and published a cautious article in the center-right national daily, Le Figaro, expressing some doubts about the original reporting.

"That image has had great influence", said Daniel Leconte, a former France 2 correspondent. "If this image does not mean what we were told, it is necessary to find the truth." [...]

For France 2, whose glass offices tower over the Seine, the nagging questions about the whole episode are a constantly shifting debate that is motivated by different agendas – from the ideology of extreme rightist groups to efforts to push Enderlin out of his Jerusalem post, where he is an institution.

When the report first aired, France 2 offered its exclusive footage for free to the world's television networks, saying it did not want to profit from the images.

The scenes were filmed by its Palestinian cameraman, Talal Abu Rahma, who was the only one to capture images of what Enderlin characterized then as the killing of a child by gunfire from the Israeli position. Enderlin was not present during the shooting.

Esther Schapira, a German producer for ARD in Frankfurt, said she tried unsuccessfully in preparation for her 2002 documentary to see a master copy of the tape and was astonished when France 2 did not share it.

European stations commonly exchange material. "If there is nothing to hide, what are they afraid of?" she said of France 2's initial reluctance.

When critical articles started appearing in publications like The Atlantic Monthly in the United States, Enderlin wrote public letters insisting: "We do not transform reality. But in view of the fact that some parts of the scene are unbearable, France 2 was obliged to cut a few seconds from the scene." [...]

Some France 2 executives privately *faulted* the channel's communication as questions were raised. Last week, they showed the International Herald Tribune the original 27-minute tape of the incident, which also includes separate scenes of rock-throwing youths.

The footage of the father and son under attack lasts several minutes but does not clearly show the child's death. There is a cut in the scene that France 2's executives attribute to the cameraman's efforts to preserve a low battery.

When Leconte and Jeambar saw the *rushes*, they were struck by the fact that there was no definitive scene that showed that the child truly died. They wrote, however, that they were not convinced that the particular scene was staged, but only that "this famous 'agony' that Enderlin insisted was cut from the montage does not exist." [...]

"It's a crazy story", said Arlette Chabot, the station's deputy general director. "Every time we address one question, then another question surfaces. It's very difficult to fight a rumor. The point is that four years later, no one can say for certain who killed him, Palestinians or Israelis." [...]

By late this weekend, Enderlin's supporters were organizing to place an advertisement in Le Monde backing the Jerusalem correspondent.

http://www.nytimes.com/2005/02/07/business/worldbusiness/07iht-video07_ed3_.htm

harrowing: extremely upsetting
indelible: permanent; sth. that cannot be extinguished
to seethe: to boil; to be violently agitated
footage: film material
"Pallywood" theater: a combination of "Palestine" and "Hollywood", i.e., a fictional Palestinian version of the event
to linger: to stay on or to remain behind
to fault: to find sth. wrong in a person or thing
rushes: (here) the first print of a film before it is edited

Tasks

1. Read the comment (M11) and complete the following tasks:
   a) Collect the statements given by different persons.
   b) Determine what the controversy is about.
   c) "... it is necessary to find the truth". Assess whether the truth can be found, giving reasons for your opinion.
2. a) Look at the photograph (M10) and note your first impressions: what you notice first, what attracts your interest, what confuses you.
   b) Describe elements of the photograph: Its subject, its portrayal, its mood.
   c) Explain the context of the photograph: The Situation in which the photograph was taken, to whom the picture was addressed, the effect of the photograph on you.
3. Use the same categories to analyse the photograph in M9 "Arrest". Finally, compare both photographs.
4. "Battle photographs have long been potent media weapons ...".
   a) Discuss, giving proof of your opinion.
   b) Find other examples for the above quotation.

Israeli-Palestinian Relations Reach a Standstill

M 12 "Israel's Security Fence"

This assessment, written by Mitchell Bard in 2010, is from the Jewish Virtual Library, an online collection dealing with Jewish history and affairs. The library is supported by the American-Israeli Cooperative Enterprise, a non-profit organization founded to strengthen ties between the USA and Israel.

After scores of suicide bombings and daily terrorist attacks against its civilians that have killed more than 850 people and wounded thousands more since September 2000, Israel's unity government decided to construct a security fence near the northern part of the pre-1967 "Green Line" between Israel and the West Bank to prevent Palestinian terrorists from infiltrating into Israeli population centers. The project has had the overwhelming support of the Israeli public which sees the barrier as vital to their security […].
Although critics have sought to portray the security fence as a kind of "Berlin Wall", it is nothing of the sort. First, unlike the Berlin Wall, the fence does not separate one people, Germans from Germans, and deny freedom to those on one side. Israel's security fence separates two peoples, Israelis and Palestinians, and offers freedom and security for both. Second, while Israelis are fully prepared to live with Palestinians, and 20 percent of the Israeli population is already Arab, it is the Palestinians who say they do not want to live with any Jews […]. Third, the fence is not being constructed to prevent the citizens of one state from escaping; it is designed solely to keep terrorists out of Israel. Finally, only a tiny fraction of the total length of the barrier (less than 3% or about 10 miles) is actually a 30 foot high concrete wall, and that is being built in three areas where it will prevent Palestinian *snipers* […]. from shooting at cars […] along the Trans-Israel Highway, one of the country's main roads. The wall also takes up less space than the other barriers, only about seven feet, so it did not have a great impact on the area where it was built. […] Most of the barrier will be a chain-link type fence […] combined with underground and long-range sensors, unmanned aerial vehicles, trenches, landmines and guard paths. Manned checkpoints will constitute the only way to travel back and forth through the fence. The barrier is altogether about 160 feet wide in most places.
The land used in building the security fence is seized for military purposes, not confiscated, and it remains the property of the owner. Legal procedures are already in place to allow every owner *to file an objection* to the seizure of their land. Moreover, property owners are offered compensation for the use of their land and for any damage to their trees. […]
The security fence does create some inconvenience to Palestinians, but it also saves lives. The deaths of Israelis caused by terror are permanent and irreversible whereas the hardships faced by the Palestinians are temporary and reversible.

www.jewishvirtuallibrary.org/jsource/Peace/fence.html [9 June 2011]

M 13 "Everyday Life in the West Bank"
An Israeli settler with his children, 2001

M 14 Israeli Barrier
Between Israeli and Palestinian settlements, 2004

M 15 The Hamas Charter

Excerpts from the Charter of the Islamic Resistance Movement (1988):

The Islamic Resistance Movement is a distinct Palestinian Movement which owes its loyalty to Allah, derives from Islam its way of life and strives to raise the banner of Allah over every inch of Palestine. Only under the shadow of Islam could the members of all religions coexist in safety and security for their lives, properties and rights. In the absence of Islam, conflict arises, oppression reigns, corruption is rampant and struggles and wars prevail […].

Article eleven

The Islamic Resistance Movement believes that the land of Palestine has been an Islamic Wakf [a charitable endowment] throughout the generations and until the Day of Resurrection, no one can renounce it or part of it, or abandon it or part of it. No Arab country nor the aggregate of all Arab countries, and no Arab King or President nor all of them in the aggregate, have that right, nor has that right any organization or the aggregate of all organizations, be they Palestinian or Arab […].

Article thirteen

[Peace] initiatives, the so-called peaceful solutions, and the international conferences to resolve the Palestinian problem, are all contrary to the beliefs of the Islamic Resistance Movement. For renouncing any part of Palestine means renouncing part of the religion; the nationalism of the Islamic Resistance Movement is part of its faith, the movement educates its members to adhere to its principles and to raise the banner of Allah over their homeland as they fight their Jihad. "Allah is the all-powerful, but most people are not aware […]".

Article thirty-two

World Zionism and Imperialism forces have been attempting, with smart moves and considered planning, to push the Arab countries, one after another, out of the circle of conflict with Zionism, in order, ultimately to isolate the Palestinian People. Egypt has already been cast out of the conflict, to a very great extent through the treacherous Camp David Accords, and she has been trying to drag other countries into similar agreements in order to push them out of the circle of conflict.

Walter Laqueur and Barry Rubin (eds.), The Israel-Arab Reader (New York: Penguin 2008), p. 341–348.

sniper: sb. who shoots from a hidden place
to file an objection: to object legally

M 16 Potential Hamas Suicide Bomber
Photograph, 2009

Tasks

1. Comment on Bard's article, including counter arguments (M12).
2. a) List the main arguments of the Hamas Charter (M15).
   b) Assess the arguments.
3. Evaluate the consequences of hardening positions in the Middle East conflict. Consider the evidence in the photographs (M13, M14).
4. Give your personal opinion on the role of religion in the Middle East conflict.

The Middle East Conflict – Analysing Works of Fiction

M 17 "To the End of the Land"

In this excerpt from David Grossman's novel of 2010, Ora and Ilan are the Israeli parents of Ofer and Adam. Avram is a family friend.

What do you tell a six-year-old boy, a pip-squeak Ofer, who one morning, while you're taking him to school, holds you close on the bike and asks in a cautious voice, "Mommy, who's against us?" And you try to find out exactly what he means, and he answers impatiently, "Who hates us in the world? Which countries are against us?" And of course you want to keep his world innocent and free of hatred, and you tell him that those who are against us don't always hate us, and that we just have a long argument with some of the countries around us about all sorts of things, just like children in school sometimes have arguments and even fights. But his little hands tighten around your stomach, and he demands the names of the countries that are against us, and there is an urgency in his voice and in his sharp chin that digs into your back, and so you start to name them: "Syria, Jordan, Iraq, Lebanon. But not Egypt – we have peace with them!" you say cheerfully. "We had lots of wars with them, but now we've made up." [...] But he demands precision, a very practical, detail-oriented child: "Is Egypt really our friend?" "Not really," you admit, "they still don't completely want to be our friends." "So they're against us," he solemnly decrees, and immediately asks if there are other "countries of Arabs," and he doesn't let up until you name them all: "Saudi Arabia, Libya, Sudan, Kuwait, and Yemen." You can feel his mouth learning the namens behind your back, and you add Iran – not exactly Arabs, but not exactly our friends, either. After a pause he asks softly if there are any more, and you mumble, "Morocco, Tunisia, Algeria," and then you remember Indonesia and Malaysia, Pakistan and Afghanistan, and probably Uzbekistan and Kazakhstan too – none of those stans sounds so great to you – and here we are at school, sweetie! When you help him get off the bike seat, he feels heavier than usual.
Over the following days Ofer started to listen closely to the news. Even if he was in the middle of a game, he would perk up just before the hour and again at the half-hour bulletin. Secretly, with spy-like movements, he would move toward the

M 18 "To the End of the Land"
Book cover

M 19 David Grossman
receives the Peace Prize of the German Book Trade in the Paulskirche in Frankfurt, Germany
Photograph,10 October 2010.

kitchen and stand, as if by chance, near the door, listening to the radio that was always on. She watched his little face twist into a mixture of anger and fear every time there was a report of an Israeli killed in an act of hostility. "Are you sad?" she asked him when he sobbed after another bomb went off in the market in Jerusalem, and he stomped his feet: "I'm not sad, I'm angry! They're killing all our people! Soon we'll run out of people!" She tried to reassure him: "We have a strong army, and there are some very big and strong countries that will protect us." Ofer treated this information with skepticism. He wanted to know where exactly these friendly countries were. Ora opened an atlas: "Here's the United States of America, for example, and here's England, and here are another few good friends of ours." She quickly waved an overgeneralizing hand near a few European countries that she herself did not particularly trust. He looked at her in astonishment. "But they're all the way over there!" he shouted, in disbelief at her stupidity. "Look how many pages there are between here and there!"
A few days later he asked her to show him the countries that were "against us." She opened up the atlas again and pointed to each country, one after the other. "Wait, but where are we?" A glimmer of hope shone in his eyes: Maybe they weren't on that page. She pointed with her pinky finger at Israel. A strange whimper escaped his lips, and he suddenly clung to her as hard as he could, fought and plowed his way to her with his whole body, as though trying to be swallowed up in it again. She hugged him and stroked him and murmured words of comfort. Sharp sweat, almost an old man's sweat, broke out all over his skin. When she managed to hold up his face, she saw in his eyes something that knotted her gut in one pull.
Over the next days he grew uncharacteristically quiet. Even Adam could not cheer him up. Ilan and Ora tried. They plied him with promises of a trip to Holland over summer vacation, or even a Kenyan safari, all in vain. He was depressed and lifeless, lost in himself. Ora realized then how much her own happiness depended on the light of this child's face.
"His gaze," said Ilan. "I don't like the look in his eyes. It's not a child's look."
"At us?"
"At everything. Haven't you noticed?"
She may have noticed, of course she'd noticed, but as usual – "You know me," she sighs as she and Avram walk down the Meron. "You know how I am with these things" – she simply preferred not to think about what she saw, to turn a blind eye to all the signs, and certainly not to say anything about them out loud, hoping they would fade away. But now Ilan would say it, he would define it, he would soberly und crudely put words to it, and then it would become real, and it would grow and multiply.
"It's like he knows something we don't yet have the courage to –"
"Don't worry about it, it's just a phase. These are normal fears at that age."
"I'm telling you Ora, they're not."
She giggled joylessly. "You remember how when Adam was three, he was really preoccupied with the question of whether there were Arabs at night, too?"
"But this is something different, Ora. My feeling is that –"
"Listen, let's take him to spend a day on the horse ranch he once –"
"Sometimes I have the feeling he's looking at us like –"
"A parrot!" Ora fluttered desperately. "Remember he asked us to buy him a –"
"Like we've been given death sentences."

David Grossman, To the End of the Land (London: Jonathan Cape, 2010), pp. S. 373–375.

Tasks

1. a) Point out the historical allusions in the excerpt from David Grossman's novel "To the End of the Land" (M17).
   b) Explain the subject of the dialogue between mother and son.
   c) Describe the mother's feelings and those of her son.
2. Imagine yourself in Israeli. A group of small children surrounds you and asks: "Who are Israel's friends and foes?" Formulate your answer.

The Israeli-Palestinian Conflict in the *Aftermath* of the "Arab Spring" in 2011

aftermath: the result of a bad event
pretext: a reason given to hide one's real intentions
to perpetrate: to do sth. harmful, dishonest or illegal

The first two years of the government of Prime Minister Benjamin Netanyahu (since 31 March 2009) were relatively quiet as far as violence between Israelis and Arabs was concerned. But no real progress was made towards peace or a lasting solution of the problems. There was, however, constant pressure on the Israeli government, especially from US President Obama.

When in 2011 unrest broke out in Arab states which had been governed by oppressive regimes for decades, the movement did not spread to Israel or the Palestinian territories. Israeli Arabs demonstrated in solidarity with their brethren in Egypt, but not against the Israeli government or its politics. Arab politicians in Israel made it clear that the protests in different parts of the Arab world did not have any impact on Arabs in Israel. Nor was there unrest or violence in the territories under Palestinian control. However, radicals used the events as a *pretext* to launch rockets from the Gaza Strip at targets in Israel. A terrorist attack on a bus station in Jerusalem in March 2011 was the first of its kind after a long period of relative calm. The killing of a family of settlers in Itamar near Nablus in March 2011 led to the announcement that 500 new housing units would be constructed in the Palestinian territories. Later it was revealed that only two Arabs had been involved in the crime *perpetrated* by an Asian worker.

It remains to be seen what will come of Netanyahu's proposed new approach to an agreement with the Palestinians. If radical Arabs engage in more hostile confrontations, he might react with tough countermeasures, as he has to compete with Foreign Minister Liberman for leadership within the right wing of the political spectrum.

M 1 "Get away"
Cartoon, 1988

President Obama's speech on the Middle East 2011

M 2 "A Choice between ... the *Shackles* of the Past and the Promise of the Future"

Excerpt from U.S. President Obama's speech on the Middle East, 19 May 2011:

For decades, the conflict between Israelis and Arabs has cast a shadow over the [Middle East] region. For Israelis, it has meant living with the fear that their children could be blown up on a bus or by rockets fired at their homes, as well as the pain of knowing that other children in the region are taught to hate them. For Palestinians, it has meant suffering the humiliation of occupation, and never living in a nation of their own. Moreover, this conflict has come with a larger *cost* to the Middle East, as it impedes partnerships that could bring greater security and prosperity and empowerment to ordinary people. [...]

At a time when the people of the Middle East and North Africa are casting off the burdens of the past, the drive for a lasting peace that ends the conflict and resolves all claims is more urgent than ever. That's certainly true for the two parties involved.

For the Palestinians, efforts *to delegitimize* Israel will end in failure. Symbolic actions to isolate Israel at the United Nations in September won't create an independent state. Palestinian leaders will not achieve peace or prosperity if Hamas insists on a path of terror and rejection. And Palestinians will never realize their independence by denying the right of Israel to exist.

As for Israel, our friendship is rooted deeply in a shared history and shared values. Our *commitment* to Israel's security is unshakeable. And we will stand against attempts to single it out for criticism in international forums. But precisely because of our friendship, it's important that we tell the truth: The status quo is *unsustainable*, and Israel too must act boldly to advance a lasting peace.

The fact is, a growing number of Palestinians live west of the Jordan River. Technology will make it harder for Israel to defend itself. A region undergoing profound change will lead to *populism* in which millions of people – not just one or two leaders – must believe peace is possible. ... What America and the international community can do is to state frankly what everyone knows – a lasting peace will involve two states for two peoples: Israel as a Jewish state and the homeland for the Jewish people, and the state of Palestine as the homeland for the Palestinian people, each state enjoying self-determination, mutual recognition, and peace.

So while the core issues of the conflict must be negotiated, the basis of those negotiations is clear: a *viable* Palestine, a secure Israel. The United States believes that negotiations should result in two states, with permanent Palestinian borders with Israel, Jordan, and Egypt, and permanent Israeli borders with Palestine. We believe the borders of Israel and Palestine should be based on the 1967 lines with mutually agreed *swaps*, so that secure and recognized borders are established for both states. The Palestinian people must have the right to govern themselves, and reach their full potential, in a sovereign and *contiguous* state.

As for security, every state has the right to self-defense, and Israel must be able to defend itself -- by itself – against any threat. Provisions must also be robust enough to prevent a resurgence of terrorism, to stop the infiltration of weapons, and to provide effective border security. The full and phased withdrawal of Israeli military forces should be coordinated with the assumption of Palestinian security responsibility in a sovereign, non-militarized state. And the duration of this transition period must be agreed, and the effectiveness of security arrangements must be demonstrated.

These principles provide a foundation for negotiations. Palestinians should know the territorial outlines of their state; Israelis should know that their basic security concerns will be

shackle: chain
cost: damage or loss
to delegitimize: not to acknowledge as legal
commitment: promise to do sth., duty or responsibility
unsustainable: not capable of being continued
populism: politics that represent the interests of the ordinary people
viable: able to live and grow independently
swap: the process of giving one thing in exchange for another
contiguous: connecting without a break

President Obama's speech on the Middle East 2011 – Reactions

met. I'm aware that these steps alone will not resolve the conflict, because two *wrenching* and emotional issues will remain: the future of Jerusalem, and the fate of Palestinian refugees. But moving forward now on the basis of territory and security provides a foundation to resolve those two issues in a way that is just and fair, and that respects the rights and aspirations of both Israelis and Palestinians.

Now, let me say this: Recognizing that negotiations need to begin with the issues of territory and security does not mean that it will be easy to come back to the table. In particular, the recent announcement of an agreement between Fatah and Hamas raises profound and legitimate questions for Israel: How can one negotiate with a party that has shown itself unwilling to recognize your right to exist? And in the weeks and months to come, Palestinian leaders will have to provide a credible answer to that question. Meanwhile, the United States, our Quartet partners, and the Arab states will need to continue every effort to get beyond the current *impasse*. [...]

[T]he choice that must be made – not simply in the Israeli-Palestinian conflict, but across the entire region – [is] a choice between hate and hope; between the shackles of the past and the promise of the future. It's a choice that must be made by leaders and by the people, and it's a choice that will define the future of a region that served as the cradle of civilization and a *crucible of strife*.

http://www.nytimes.com/2011/05/20/world/middleeast/20prexy-text.html [25 May 2011]

M 3 "Israel will not return to the indefensible lines of 1967"

Excerpt from Israeli Prime Minister Benjamin Netanyahu's speech to a joint session of the U.S. Congress, 24 May 2011:

[Any Israeli-Palestinian] compromise must reflect the dramatic demographic changes that have occurred since 1967. The vast majority of the 650,000 Israelis who live beyond the 1967 lines, reside in neighborhoods and suburbs of Jerusalem and Greater Tel Aviv.

These areas are densely populated but geographically quite small. Under any realistic peace agreement, these areas, as well as other places of critical strategic and national importance, will be incorporated into the final borders of Israel.

The status of the settlements will be decided only in negotiations. But we must also be honest. [...] In any peace agreement that ends the conflict, some settlements will end up beyond Israel's borders. The precise delineation of those borders must be negotiated. We will be very generous on the size of a future Palestinian state. But as President Obama said, the border will be different than the one that existed on June 4, 1967. Israel will not return to the indefensible lines of 1967.

We recognize that a Palestinian state must be big enough to be viable, independent and prosperous. President Obama rightly referred to Israel as the homeland of the Jewish people, just as he referred to the future Palestinian state as the homeland of the Palestinian people. Jews from around the world have a right to immigrate to the Jewish state. Palestinians from around the world should have a right to immigrate, if they so choose, to a Palestinian state. This means that the Palestinian refugee problem will be resolved outside the borders of Israel.

As for Jerusalem, only a democratic Israel has protected freedom of worship for all faiths in the city. Jerusalem must never again be divided. Jerusalem must remain the united capital of Israel. I know that this is a difficult issue for Palestinians. But I believe with creativity and goodwill a solution can be found.

This is the peace I plan *to forge* with a Palestinian partner committed to peace. But you know very well, that in the Middle East, the only peace that will hold is a peace you can defend. [...] The truth is that Israel needs unique security arrangements because of its unique size. Israel is one of the smallest countries in the world. [...] But Israel on the 1967 lines would be only nine miles wide. [...] So it is therefore absolutely vital for Israel's security that a Palestinian state be fully demilitarized. And it is vital that Israel maintain a long-term military presence along the Jordan River. Solid security arrangements on the ground are necessary not only to protect the peace, they are necessary to protect Israel in case the peace *unravels*. For in our unstable region, no one can guarantee that our peace partners today will be there tomorrow.

http://communities.canada.com/shareit/blogs/news/archive/2011/05/24/full-text-of-benjamin-netanyahu-s-speech-to-congress-may-24.aspx [25 May 2011]

M 4 **"Palestinians: Netanyahu speech to U.S. Congress is obstacle to peace"**

Excerpt from Haaretz (Israeli newspaper), 24 May 2011:

"What came in Netanyahu's speech will not lead to peace," Nabil Abu Rdainah, the spokesman for Palestinian President Mahmoud Abbas, told Reuters following Netanyahu's address to the U.S. Congress on Wednesday. [...]

Chief Palestinian negotiator Saeb Erekat *slammed* the prime minister's speech, saying it was "full of lies" and "distorted history and geography."

MK Ahmed Tibi said that Netanyahu "misled" the Congress members by describing Israel as a place where Arabs are equal citizens.

"There is not one are[a] where there is equality between Jews and Arabs", Tibi said.

Palestinians have said that they will meet in Ramallah on Wednesday to determine what their next step will be, following Netanyahu's visit to Washington.

http://www.haaretz.com/news/diplomacy-defense/palestinians-netanyahu-speech-to-u-s-congress-is-obstacle-to-peace-1.363859 [25 May 2011]

M 5 **Palestinian Reactions**

The news agency Reuters reported on Palestinian reactions to Obama's and Netanyahu's speeches, 25 May 2011:

Palestinian President Mahmoud Abbas said Israel was offering "nothing we can build on" for peace and that without progress he will seek U.N. recognition of Palestinian statehood in September.

He told the Palestine Liberation Organization on Wednesday that Israeli Prime Minister Benjamin Netanyahu's speech to the United States Congress on Tuesday "travelled far from peace", dictating solutions before negotiations even begin. [...]

He said he would consult Arab states at the weekend about U.S. President Barack Obama's latest ideas for restarting the peace process and Netanyahu's negative response to them.

"We said in the past and we still say that our choice is negotiation, negotiation and nothing but negotiation. But if nothing happens by September we will go (to the U.N. to ask for recognition by its 192 member states)", Abbas said.

"Our aim is not to isolate (Israel) or to de-legitimise it. It is not an act of terror and not a *unilateral* act."

Abbas's plan to seek U.N. recognition was criticised by both Netanyahu and Obama in speeches in Washington last week. [...]

Hamas leader in Gaza Ismail Haniyeh said Netanyahu's speech revealed "the real face of the occupation [...] the real face of arrogance backed by the Americans."

"We must quit this illusion called negotiation", he said.

http://www.reuters.com/article/2011/05/25/us-israel-palestinians-idUSTRE74O2RB20110525 [26 May 2011]

to wrench: to pull or twist violently
impasse: standstill
crucible of strife: (here) severe test or ordeal determined by conflict
to forge: to mould (to make)
to unravel: to undo, to come apart
to slam: (here) to criticize severely
unilateral: decided by one side alone

Tasks

1. Analyse these recent developments (text, M1 – M5) in terms of how new or old the positions are.
2. List your findings in a table with two columns.
3. Evaluate your results in a class discussion.
4. Newspapers, radio and television report on the Middle East very often. Consider how the information and activities from this unit on the "Conflict in Middle East" have helped you to understand the history and current situation of the Israelis and Palestinians better.
5. Write your personal feedback to the publisher.

Summary

The Middle East conflict has functioned as a common theme in the second half of the 20th century. It has been a constant topic of world politics in the past and the present. No conflict has provoked so many wars and so many numerous and intensive peace initiatives at the highest levels.

The constants of the conflict have been remarkably stable:

- Irreconcilability of the interests of the conflicting parties: Both demand essentially the same territory; both sides have minorities which cannot give in.
- Lack of compromise on both sides: Negotiations fail again and again due to details on which no compromise is possible.
- Involvement of powers outside of the region such as Great Britain, France, the Soviet Union, the USA, EU, UN, etc.
- Attempts to solve the conflict from outside the region: The UN, EU, Soviet Union, USA, various US Presidents have all started initiatives; the "Middle East Quartet", which actively supports peace, consists of the USA, Russia, the UN and EU.
- Implications: Oil (Arab embargo after the October War of 1973), international traffic routes (closing of the Straits of Tiran), stability of the Mediterranean region, regional development potential
- Danger of escalation: Arab involvement (in the earlier conflict), Iranian involvement (today).

On the one hand, the Middle East conflict is a historical development which extends far back in history and can only be explained in light of it. On the other hand, the conflict remains ceaselessly current. It will play an essential role in international relations in the future, as no resolution is in sight either in the near or mid-term future. Unlike nearly any other conflict in world history, it is emotionally laden not only for those directly involved, but also in the arena of world opinion.

Literature

W. Laqueur / B. Rubin, The Israel-Arab Reader, New York 2008.

David Grossman, To the End of the Land, London 2010.

Amira Hass, Drinking the Sea at Gaza: Days and Nights in a Land under Siege, New York 2000.

A. Shlaim, The Iron Wall. Israel and the Arab World, New York 2001.

"The Conflict in the Middle East"
Cartoon by Fritz Behrendt

Timeline

113th century B.C.	Jews settle in Palestine (late Bronze Age)
6th century B.C.	Jewish "Babylonian captivity"
70 A.D.	Romans destroy the Jewish temple in Jerusalem, Judea becomes a Roman province
634	Arab-Muslim conquest of Palestine
1095	Pope Urban II calls for the First Crusade ("God wills it!")
1099	Crusaders conquer Jerusalem
1291	Acre, last bastion of the Crusaders, falls
1897	First Zionist Congress in Basel
1915	McMahon Letter
1916	Sykes-Picot Agreement
1917	Balfour Declaration
1933	National Socialist assumption of power in Germany
1948/49	Israeli Declaration of Independence – First Arab-Israeli War
1956	Suez Crisis (Israel, France, Great Britain against Egypt)
1964	Palestine Liberation Organization (PLO) founded
1967	"Six-Day War": Israel occupies East Jerusalem, the West Bank, Golan Heights and Gaza Strip
1973 October	"Yom Kippur" or "Ramadan" War
1978/79	Camp David Accords: Israel-Egypt Peace Treaty
1981	Assassination of Egyptian President Sadat
1982	Israeli invasion of Lebanon
1987	Hamas founded
1987–1993	First Intifada (= uprising)
1993–1995	"Oslo Process": Accords on Palestinian Autonomy
1994	Peace between Israel and Jordan
1995	Assassination of Israeli Prime Minister Rabin
2000–2005	Second ("Temple Mount") Intifada
2005	Armistice of Sharm el-Sheikh (Israel, Palestinian Autonomy Authority); Israeli Prime Minister Ariel Sharon forces Jewish settlers to leave the Gaza Strip
2006	Hamas wins elections in the Palestinian territories
2008/2009	Gaza War (Israeli "Operation Cast Lead")
2009 March	Prime Minister Benjamin Netanyahu
2011	"Arab Spring"
2011 May	President Obama´s speech on the Middle East

A Compendium of Historical Methods

History relies not only on facts, but even more on the analysis of relevant materials. Most important are sources, those remains that inform us about the past. Written documents, pictures, and objects make up different categories of sources. In addition, students of history have to be able to read historical maps and evaluate statistics correctly.

Working with Written Documents

Primary sources are centrally important in historical research. They can be notes, diaries, or memoirs, as well as literary works, speeches, or political programmes and were written when the events under study occurred. Because these documents are so different, historians have to adapt their questions and procedures to the document under study. However, there are some basic rules of analysis which are relevant for all these sources.

Secondary sources, such as historical accounts or textbooks, sum up the results found in the primary sources and present them to the interested public. Older secondary works can become primary sources themselves when, for example, historians want to know how people, events, or developments were interpreted in earlier times.

The scheme offered here can also be used to interpret such secondary sources, as the source type and its intended audience have already been identified.

Procedure and questions for interpreting written documents

1. Read the text and understand its content	- What kind of document is it? - What is the subject? - What do unknown terms mean? - What is the central statement? ...
2. Establish the origins and background of the text	- When was it written? - Who wrote it? - How was it passed on to us? - Was the text shortened or revised? - Are there other comparable sources? ...
3. Explain the context of the text and what it refers to historically	- In what situation did the document play a role? - Whom did the document address? - What effect did it have? - What allusions can be found to the historical situation? ...
4. Interpret the text in summary	- How important was the source in the situation? - How important is the source for our knowledge of the situation? - Is the source supported by other sources? ...

Working with Pictures and Objects

It took a while for pictures to interest historians, but in more recent times they have become increasingly important. In the 20th century photography played an eminent role, but pictorial documents include prehistoric cave paintings as well as 3D simulations, paintings, posters, caricatures and even comics. In film photographs – so-called stills – the transition is relative. The procedure and questions below must be adapted according to the type of picture being analysed.

In principle the same procedure also applies to objects, which come in even more variations than pictures. An object can be a bone found at a site or even a historical monument. In the case of a monument, a written and pictorial source may also be included as part of it. Of course, its location must also be taken into account.

Procedure and questions for interpreting pictures

1. Take in the picture and describe your first impression	- What is the mood of the picture? - What do you notice first? - What attracts your interest? - What confuses you? ...
2. Establish the origins and the background of the picture	- When and how was the picture made? - How large is it? - Are you looking at the original, a copy, or a detail of it? - How was it passed on to us? - Are there comparable pictures? ...
3. Describe the elements of the picture	- What in particular is shown? - How is it portrayed? - What can be seen where in the picture? ...
4. Decode the elements of the picture	- Who are the figures (if present) portrayed? - What do the colours suggest? - What does the structure of the picture suggest? ...
5. Explain the context of the picture and what it refers to historically	- What was the situation in which the picture played a role? - Whom did the picture address? - What effect did it have? - What allusions can be found to the historical situation? ...
6. Interpret the picture in summary	- How important was the picture in the situation? - How important is the picture for our knowledge of the situation? - Is the picture supported by other sources? ...

Working with Maps

Just like other types of sources, maps can be separated into primary and secondary sources. Historic maps, which were made in earlier times, are primary sources and reveal what people at the time knew or thought about their surroundings. Historical maps are secondary sources. They show results that researchers have determined in cartographic form. In addition to providing geographic orientation, historical maps can provide a wealth of information, such as events, territorial changes or trade relations. Interpreted correctly, these maps offer valuable insight on times past. Historical maps can themselves become historic. For example, wall maps made before the unification of Germany reflect the division of the country and the Cold War.

Procedure and questions for interpreting maps

1. Look at the map carefully and get your bearings

- What is the subject of the map?
- Which map excerpt has been chosen?
- What is the scale of the map?
- What is in the legend?

...

2. Establish the origins and the background of the map

- When was the map made?
- Who made it?
- How was it passed on?
- Are there other comparable sources?

...

3. Determine the content of the map

- What sort of map is it (economic, political, etc.)?
- What period of time does it refer to?
- Is it a static map, showing a state of affairs, or a dynamic map, showing a development?
- Which regions are shown?

...

4. Consider the map critically

- Does the use of colour have a specific effect?
- If a different excerpt is chosen, does it change the impression created?
- How is the title or heading formulated?

...

5. Interpret the map in a summary

- How important was the map in the situation?
- How important is the map for our knowledge of the historical situation?

...

Working with Statistics

Columns of figures, bills, and balance sheets have been passed down to posterity for centuries, so they can also be considered written sources. The systematic collection, preparation, and interpretation of data are achievements of the "statistical age" which began in the 19th century. Statistics from earlier times are mostly based on estimates. Older statistics can certainly be seen as sources, while more recent statistics on historical developments have usually been compiled from contemporary data. Various forms of presentation are possible, from tables to graphs and complex diagrams.

The procedure and questions used in interpreting statistics are given below. However, these must be adapted to the specific type of statistics under study.

Procedure and questions for interpreting statistics

1. Look at the statistics carefully and determine their principles
- What is the subject of the statistics?
- Which form of presentation has been chosen?
- What data are the statistics based on?
- What do the terms used in the statistics mean?

...

2. Establish the origins and background of the statistics
- When were the statistics made?
- Who made them?
- How were they passed on to us?
- Are there comparable statistics available?

...

3. Determine the content of the statistics
- What period of time do the statistics refer to?
- Which data are shown and which are put in relation to each other?
- Which units of measurement are used?

...

4. Consider the statistics critically
- Is the sample size sufficient?
- Are the values valid?
- Are important aspects missing?
- Is the chosen time period convincing?
- Is the graphic presentation acceptable?

...

5. Interpret the statistics in summary
- How important were the statistics in the situation?
- How important are the statistics for our knowledge of the situation?
- Are the findings of the statistics supported by other sources?

...

War and peace
to be responsible for the outbreak of the war
to set off / trigger a war
to enter / join the war
to declare war
to win / lose a battle / war
to occupy / take control of / invade / annex / conquer a country / territory
to mobilize / demobilize troops / an army
to demand / pay reparations
to establish peace / to stabilize a country
to prevent a military conflict
to conquer territory
to expand a sphere of influence
to invade a country
to support the war effort
to surrender unconditionally / to demand unconditional surrender
on the brink of war
to reach a target
to set up / to station / to install missiles / weapons
to launch a missile / rocket / nuclear strike
to supply sb. with weapons
to withdraw (troops) from
to station
to pay / negotiate / reduce reparations
to make / default on reparations payments
to comply with conditions of a treaty
to fight a proxy war
to use military force / to resort to coercion
to advance / withdraw an army / soldiers
to occupy a zone

Diplomacy
to send / serve as an ambassador / (an envoy)
to have / break off diplomatic relations with a country
to achieve a diplomatic triumph
to guarantee neutrality
to negotiate / sign an agreement / a pact / a treaty
to stir up / settle a dispute over

Diplomacy
to cause / create rising tensions
to issue / deliver an ultimatum
to sign / negotiate an armistice / a peace treaty
to proclaim a republic
to ratify / revise a treaty
to order / announce a plebiscite
to establish an international order
to appease / pacify / stand up to a dictator
to pose a threat to sb.
to confront sb.
sphere of influence
to be dependent on
to be politically linked to
to reassure sb.
to blockade a country
to lift a blockade
to put up an embargo
to urge sb. to do sth.
to pursue a policy of rapprochement / aggression

Economy
to invest money / to go bankrupt
to increase production
to exploit natural resources / exploitation
to open new markets
to be employed / unemployed / a skilled / unskilled worker
to enjoy economic benefits
to suffer from food shortages
to benefit from measures
to battle / decrease unemployment
to provide work / create jobs
to increase sb.'s living standard
to introduce a new currency / currency reform
to barter / exchange goods
to draw / receive a pension / salary
to institute austerity measures
to prime the economy
to raise taxes / to cut benefits / expenses
to restrict trade / the exchange of goods

Human Rights
to demand / to guarantee civil rights / human rights
to fight for your rights
to ask for / demand the right to work / freedom of speech / of assembly / of political union / of religion / of the press / of property
to support / demand / grant universal / women's suffrage
to extend voting rights to …
to violate civil rights
to restrict / allow political activities
to censor the press
to relax / remove press censorship
to persecute sb.
to persecute a minority / to mark social outcasts
to discriminate against sb.
to become a victim of persecution
to exclude sb. from society
to blame sb. for sth.
to isolate a group in ghettos
to exterminate sb.
to sentence to death
to be sent into exile
to be imprisoned / arrested
to formulate basic rights and obligations
to abuse / mistreat / torture civilians / soldiers / prisoners of war
to resettle displaced persons
to commit genocide

Law and constitution
to pass / enact / initiate / oppose a law
to obey / break / abolish a law / act
to write / ratify a constitution
to open / dissolve a national assembly
to send a deputy / representative to parliament
to have a free / imperative mandate
to approve / reject the budget
to call for (new) elections
to appoint sb. chancellor / to elect sb. to parliament
to gain the right

Law and constitution
to entrust an office / an official with powers
to appoint / dismiss a government / judges / officials
to determine the direction of policy
to hold a referendum / plebiscite / initiative
to take / suspend a measure
to rescind an edict
to pass a vote of no confidence
to pass a constructive vote of no confidence
to rule by decree / by parliamentary majority

Domestic policy / Living conditions
to experience upward mobility / fear social decline
to be a member of the upper / middle / lower class
to be a second- / third-class citizen
to become rich / poor / homeless / disabled
to live in poverty / to starve (to death)
to own land / property
to suffer in / from a famine
to provide health / accident / old-age insurance
to appeal to voters
to consolidate (its) power
to introduce an act / a law
to eliminate opponents
to ban political parties
to transform democracy into a dictatorship
to execute control over sb.
to indoctrinate sb.
to distribute leaflets
to resist sb.
to overthrow a regime
to participate in a plot
to assassinate a dictator
to set up a provisional government
to establish councils of workers and soldiers
to encourage plebiscitary participation
to call for / begin a general strike
to enact reforms

akg images, Berlin: 4 top left + centre right, 6 M1, 7 M3, 13 M11 (British Library), 15 M2
Associated Press, Frankfurt/M.: 34 M13 (B. Hendler)

Baaske Cartoons, Müllheim: 4 centre left + 16 M4 (F. Behrendt), 38 M1 (G. Mester), 42 bottom (F. Behrendt)

Getty Images, München: 35 M16 (C. Kealy)

Jonathan Cape, London: 36 M18

Langner + Partner, Hemmingen: 22 M7

Magnum Photos Inc., New York: 20 M5

Picture Alliance, Frankfurt/M.: Title + 4 bottom right + 28 M6 (AFP/S. Nackstrand), 4 bottom left (dpa/F. Nureline), 18 M1 (dpa), 18 M2 (KPA/TopFoto), 25 M1 (Consolidated), 26 M2 (SVEN SIMON), 26 M3 (AFP), 31 M9 (AFP), 32 M10 (AFP/J. Barrak), 36 M19 (dpa/F. Rumpenhorst)

Schoenfeld, K.-H., Potsdam: 27 M4
Süddeutsche Zeitung Photo, München: 19 M3 (AP), 19 M4

ullsteinbild, Berlin: 21 M6 (SIPA)

Weigand, W., München: 8 M4, 9 M5, 11 M8

all other diagrams and maps: Westermann Kartographie/Technisch Graphische Abteilung, Braunschweig